Essential

2.50

Thailand

by
CHRISTINE OSBORNE

Christine Osborne is an award-winning writer
who has travelled widely in the near and far
east researching and photographing for
numerous books and articles. Her knowledge
of Thailand is unsurpassed and has been
gained over many years.

D1396204

AA

Produced by AA Publishing

Written by Christine Osborne
Peace and Quiet section
by Paul Sterry

Edited, designed and produced
by AA Publishing. Maps ©
The Automobile Association 1994

Distributed in the United Kingdom
by AA Publishing, Norfolk House,
Priestley Road, Basingstoke,
Hampshire, RG24 9NY.

The contents of this publication are
believed correct at the time of
printing. Nevertheless, the publishers
cannot be held responsible for any
errors or omissions, or for changes in
details given in this guide or for the
consequences of any reliance on the
information provided by the same.
Assessments of attractions, hotels,
restaurants and so forth are based
upon the author's own experience
and, therefore, descriptions given in
this guide necessarily contain an
element of subjective opinion which
may not reflect the publisher's opinion
or dictate a reader's own experience
on another occasion.
**We have tried to ensure accuracy
in this guide, but things do change
and we would be grateful if readers
would advise us of any inaccuracies
they may encounter.**

First published 1990
Revised second edition © The
Automobile Association 1994
Reprinted November 1994

A CIP catalogue record for this book
is available from the British Library.

ISBN 0 7495 0842 6

Published by AA Publishing, which is
a trading name of Automobile
Association Developments Limited,
whose registered office is Norfolk
House, Priestley Road, Basingstoke,
Hampshire, RG24 9NY.
Registered number 1878835.

Colour separation: Mullis Morgan
Ltd., London

Printed by: Printers Trento, S.R.L.,
Italy

Cover picture: Bankok

COUNTRY DISTINGUISHING SIGNS
On some maps, international distinguishing signs have been used to indicate the location of the countries which surround Thailand.

=Burma
=Kampuchea
=Laos
=Malaysia
=Vietnam

MAPS AND PLANS
Southeast Asia	4
Thailand	6
Bangkok	26
Phuket	77

This book employs a simple rating system to help choose which places to visit:

✓	'top ten'

♦♦♦   do not miss
♦♦   see if you can
♦   worth seeing if you have time

The abbreviation TAT stands for the Tourism Authority of Thailand

INTRODUCTION

It is easy to see why Thailand has become the most popular tourist destination in Southeast Asia. Visually stunning, it sums up quixotic images of everyman's Asia: gilded temples, lush paddy-fields, exotic foods and gracious, smiling people. 'Land of Smiles' is a common description of Thailand, whose society draws deeply on its rich, cultural background. 'Land of the Free' is an equally appropriate epithet for this beautiful country of 56.9 million people. Wherever you go, dazzling scenes from *The King and I* appear and disappear: fruit-laden market boats on languid canals (*khlongs*), bejewelled dancers, caparisoned elephants, fluttering kites and craftsmen producing artistic masterpieces from teak and enamel. Thailand exudes a dream-like quality that alternately

excites and soothes. Tourists who only visit the capital, however, may not agree. In a sense they are right. It is merely that Bangkok's treasures – the Grand Palace compound is incomparable – are lost in noise, pollution and some of the world's worst traffic jams. Some say the city is sinking into the mud: you can even buy a car-sticker which reads 'I Survived the Bangkok Floods'.

But the cosmopolitan face of Bangkok, seat of government and centre of commerce, is no reflection of the rest of Thailand. Eighty per cent of Thais are engaged in agriculture of some sort: rice- and fruit-growing, duck-farming and fishing. To obtain an overall picture of the country, you must therefore travel quite extensively from the hilly north across the alluvial central plains to the deep south and the offshore islands. These regions are as different from Bangkok and each other as eating *tom yum kung* soup with and without the addition of chillies.

Today Thailand plays host – perhaps hostess is more accurate – to more than three million visitors a year. Tourism provides employment at all levels and it has overtaken tin and rubber as the largest source of foreign exchange. Visitor demand has injected a new vigour into fragile cottage industries: until recently traditional crafts such as *yan lipao*, or fern basketry, were dying skills. Some souvenirs are mass produced, but most Thai handicrafts are works of art. There have been several violent incidents involving tourists travelling in vulnerable border areas of Thailand. Too many young travellers find the element of risk exciting. Life is cheap in any developing country and Thailand is no exception. Heed local warnings of danger. Deposit valuables in a hotel safe. Do not travel after dark in suspect regions such as the Golden Triangle, or remote islands. Thailand is basically a gentle society but never let down your guard. Images of Thailand linger long after your return home, where western ways seem, frankly, rough by comparison. Permeating every aspect of the Thai way of life, Buddhism – professed religion of the majority of Thais – has something to do with it.

BACKGROUND

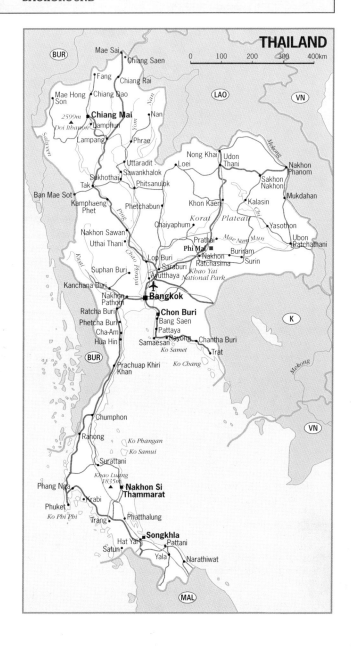

BACKGROUND

See page 124 for a short glossary of Thai words

History

Thailand's history is characterised by its cherished independence. While its neighbours were successively colonised by France and Britain, Thailand alone managed to preserve its identity. The first true capital was Sukhothai (1238–1358), the second, Ayutthaya (1358–1767); Bangkok is the country's third capital. Sukhothai reached its zenith under King Ramkhamaeng, who is credited with many achievements. Most notably he invented the Thai alphabet based on ancient Khmer scripts. An accomplished statesman, he forged cultural and economic links with other Asian countries. Chinese artisans who emigrated to Sukhothai introduced new skills. The subtle Chinese influence in Thai cooking probably dates from this time.

For 400 years, Ayutthaya was the glorious second capital of Siam, a prosperous island city known as the 'Baghdad of the East', which merchants and travellers reported was even larger than London. Foreign artists, dancers and musicians were brought to court and further enriched indigenous Thai culture.

Following the destruction of Ayutthaya, a third capital was founded in Thonburi, on the west bank of the Chao Phraya river in Bangkok. In 1782, Rama I – the first Thai monarch – transferred the capital across the river to a small site called 'Ban Kok' – village of wild plums. Successive monarchs steered Thailand clear of troubled waters. Immortalised in the Hollywood movie *The King and I,* King Mongkut, Rama IV (1851–1868) is remembered for his diplomacy when foreign powers were active in Southeast Asia. Well read and widely travelled, King Mongkut spent 27 years as a monk before becoming head of state. On his orders canals were dug and roads built, laying the basis of a national infrastructure. King Mongkut established Thailand's first mint. He sought European advice on the organisation of government services and was active in restoring many national treasures.

His son, King Chulalongkorn, Rama V (1868–1910), made two sweeping changes to society, abolishing slavery and removing the odious rule requiring commoners to prostrate themselves in his presence. His birthday, 23 October, is a national holiday. On 24 June 1932, a bloodless coup replaced the absolute monarchy with a constitutional one.

Thailand has a bicameral parliamentary system with a 100-seat appointed Senate and an elected House of Representatives. The present constitutional monarch is His Majesty King Bhumiphol Adulyadej, Rama IX, ninth monarch of the Chakri dynasty, who acceded to the throne in 1946. He speaks several foreign languages and is an accomplished musician, artist and sailor. His wife, Queen Sirikit, studied classical piano in Europe. Both monarchs are hard working, making frequent trips around their country. King Bhumiphol pioneered a system of land reform releasing 20,000 acres (81,000ha) of Crown Land to farmers. He is particularly concerned with upgrading farming and fishing techniques. The status of the hill tribes and the sustenance of ancient folk arts are royal priorities.

Religion and Society

Ninety per cent of Thais follow the Hinayana school of orthodox Buddhism, introduced in the 3rd century BC. Its teachings quickly replaced local animistic beliefs, yet aspects of animism and Hinduism surface in many customs, such as the traditional Thai wedding ceremony and the spirit house; Brahmin priests also officiate at the annual Royal Ploughing Ceremony in Bangkok.

Although traditionally and legally the king must be a Buddhist, he is also the upholder of all religions professed by his peoples.

Muslims, mainly of the Sunni school of Islam, constitute the second largest religious community. They live mainly in southern Thailand. Christians number about 300,000.

In its most simple form, Buddhism teaches 'do unto others'; while parallels exist with Christianity, it is classified as atheist as there is no God. The 'Dhamma', or discourse preached by Buddha, is known universally as the 'Four Noble Truths'. Embracing one's physical and spiritual reaction to being, they are central to Buddhist philosophy, and have a profound influence on the development of the Thai character.

Monks go out at dawn to receive food from devout almsgivers, who thus earn merit towards their advancement

Like other Buddhists, Thais believe that life on earth is merely the worldly chapter of a continuous cycle of birth and death. By meritorious actions, one can improve one's station at the next reincarnation. It is of paramount importance to accrue 'points' towards this advancement. Men can advance by becoming monks. Buddhist monks are renowned for their spiritual knowledge, self-restraint and chaste life. A small, breakaway movement from orthodox Buddhism in Bangkok known as Santi Asoke espouses vegetarianism and total abstention from sex throughout life.

In addition to the five cardinal rules for the laity – abstention from murder, adultery, stealing, telling falsehoods, or drinking intoxicating liquor – monks must observe a further 227 rules. They must walk everywhere as motorised transport is forbidden. Their only possessions are a saffron robe and an alms bowl. Contact with women is forbidden. Traditionally, every male Thai over 20 must enter a *wat* for at least three months' study and meditation. *Khao Phansa,* or Buddhist Lent, is the usual time, at the start of the rainy season. It is said that Buddha considered this a good idea as it meant less likelihood of people trampling on the new rice plants. Women can advance by preparing food for the incumbent monks. In the early morning you will see monks making food rounds all over Thailand. A good spot to watch this is outside Bangkok's Marble Temple, about 07.00hrs.

The act of buying, then releasing, captive creatures is also considered meritorious. People selling birds, tortoises and fish are found outside many temples and shrines. Wealthy people pay dancers to perform around the Erawan shrine in Bangkok, which is garlanded with flower chains and its statues gilded with gold leaf. Incense is also burned. Another quick route to Nirvana is to sponsor repairs to a *wat.* And worthy is he who builds a new *wat.* Thailand has more than 27,000 *wats,* or Buddhists monasteries. Usually found on the outskirts of a village, the shady, walled compound encloses a group of buildings whose architecture is uniquely Thai. The main chapel, or *bot,* with a glistening, multi-tiered roof, is used for religious ceremonies. Similarly embellished, a secondary chapel, or *viharn,* is used for meetings and meditations. *Chedis* or *stupas* are pagoda-type structures often containing religious relics and ashes. The open-sided *sala* is a wooden pavilion used for meditation and funeral obsequies.

The *bot* houses the altar of worship with one, or many images of the Buddha. These may be huge, like the Reclining Buddha in Bangkok's Wat Pho, or minute, like the Crystal Buddha in Chiang Mai. Images may be stone, bronze, teak, jade or even solid gold. People make offerings of flowers, food and incense to the Buddha in their village *wat.* But *wats* are not solely places for monastic learning. Schools and hospitals are often attached to them and they may have accommodation for poor students, travellers and, in some cases, delinquents. (See Wat Tham Krabok, page 46.) Animistic practices continue to surface in the Thai interpretation of Buddhism. Both men and women wear charms and amulets: a Thai businessman many wear a gold chain, a Thai boxer a cord around his arm. Like the Greek 'eye' such items are believed to keep evil at bay. By nature superstitious, Thais undertake nothing of consequence without consulting their horoscope; weddings, or moving house are only arranged if the stars are auspicious. An astrologist or palmist – usually Chinese – is always found under a shady tree in the temple compound. Neither are the spirits forgotten. Those cute little houses are not a Thai version of the garden gnome, but the abode of Phra Plum, Lord of the House. Everything has a spirit house – home, hospital, hotel, office block and shopping centre. They are erected on a pole out

of range of the building's shadow: the spirit won't take up residence within a shadow. Every day people place offerings of rice, fruit, flowers and small carved animals on the tiny terrace around their spirit house.

Buddhism and Hinduism are one in many instances. The spirit house of the demolished Erawan Hotel was erected to bring good fortune to its staff and guests. Dedicated to Brahma, for some reason over the years, it has become enormously popular with the general public. Erawan being the triple-headed elephant of Thai mythology, carved wooden elephants are common gifts. There is another large spirit house outside the River City shopping complex. People living by the water erect a spirit house in the *khlong*. Other local shrines consist of a single, phallic pillar whose significance is obvious. The Lakmuang shrine outside the

River cruises are a good way of seeing everyday life; many Thais use waterways as highways

BACKGROUND

Ministry of Defence in Bangkok is worshipped by both men and women.

Thai women are renowned for their beauty, grace and a classic Oriental subservience to men. Fortunately, the latter is limited to domestic issues since, fragile though they appear, Thai women are no fools at business. A bus company and a fleet of ferries in Bangkok are run by women. A woman owns the Dusit Thani hotel chain and many other hotels are managed by women. A former flower seller in Chiang Mai now runs a multi-million baht antiques business. A dance hostess has become proprietor of a country whore-house complete with golf course.

The Thais place great emphasis on tolerance, which is why they turn a blind eye to a *farang,* or foreigner's manners and dress. Unless overtly painful to him the Thai smiles and says nothing. Offensive dress worn in a *wat* is the most likely thing to provoke a reaction. Always neatly dressed, Thais are very fastidious in their personal habits.

People of both sexes greet each other with the *wai,* raising the palms as if in prayer. The higher they are held, the more respectful the salutation. Thais especially appreciate foreigners observing this custom. Pointing the feet at someone is considered a great affront. This includes pointing the soles of your feet at a Buddha. For your part, do not be offended by Thai curiosity about personal things such as your marital status or salary: the person is only being

friendly. It is still very unusual for someone not to marry in Thailand, although there is an increasing gay population. *Mai pen rai* is a common phrase. Roughly translated it means 'no worries – stay cool'. However, most of the time it's too hot to get excited anyway.

Land and Climate

Thailand covers an area of Southeast Asia slightly smaller than France. Boxed in between Burma, Laos and Cambodia, with a long isthmus to Malaysia, it displays four fairly distinct regions: the northern hill tracts, an arid northeast plateau, and an alluvial central plain tapering into the tropical south. A wide variety of birdlife is found where there is tree-cover. Centuries of hunting have greatly depleted animal life. Small herds of elephant still inhabit the jungle, but the Asian rhinoceros is almost extinct. Deer, wild pig, and monkeys and squirrels are common. Butterflies there are in hundreds, and thousands of varieties of orchid.

The most important river, the Chao Phraya, flows across the central plain to the Gulf of Thailand. Its delta is criss-crossed by hundreds of tributaries and man-made canals, which irrigate the rice-fields and play a traditional role in transport.

Thailand's climate is basically hot, very hot, and hot and wet. Average temperatures are about 84°F (29°C), ranging in Bangkok from 96°F (35.5°C) in April to 63°F (17°C) in December. The isthmus experiences a more consistent, equatorial-type climate. Here seasonal variations are subtle. The weather is generally warm, humid and sunny with frequent rainfall.

No sensible person visits the country during March and April when even Thais complain of the excessive heat and humidity. The saving grace is that all first-class hotels, coaches and shops are cooled by air-conditioning. While storms are characteristic of the monsoon season (June to October), temperatures are a relatively pleasant 86–91°F (30–33°C). Then the general lack of tourists compensates for grey days and occasional downpours, usually at night. Many establishments offer reduced low season rates. Travel to the islands may be affected by adverse weather. The best time of the year, November to February,

coincides with the high tourist season. Then most of the country is as cool as it ever gets in Thailand; you will even need a sweater for the north.

The Economy

Traditionally agrarian, today Thailand has a booming, multi-faceted economy. While agriculture employs two-thirds of the population, it contributes only a third of the domestic product. The manufacturing and tourism sectors are of increasing importance: more than 3 million visitors come each year.

Most factories are sited in the Bangkok conurbation. They process a number of goods ranging from foodstuffs, wood products and furniture, to metals and textiles. Traditional gem-cutting remains an important secondary industry. The newer, ready-made clothes industry is proving competitive with established Asian markets. Grown mainly in the central plain, rice is the main export crop. Combining rice-growing, poultry-raising, fish and prawn culture, integrated farming obtains maximum productivity from small holdings – the average size is 25 acres (10ha). Grain and droppings fall through the floor of the duck-house feeding the fish in the pond below, while fish swimming in the rice paddies are netted when the fields are drained at harvest time. Thailand harvests two rice crops a year. Fruits, maize and sugar-cane are also important. It is the world's largest exporter of tapioca, second largest of

Mass-produced textiles: cheap and cheerful

rubber, fifth largest of teak and sixth in the league of coconut producers. Tobacco, cotton, coffee and orchids are also significant. Commercial fishing centres on the Gulf of Thailand. Shrimp, squid and processed seafoods make a major contribution to the economy.

Rice is harvested by hand twice yearly: the yield depends on the monsoon

Modern Thailand

Change has not weakened centuries of Buddhist traditions, but while remaining profoundly philosophic, Thailand has moved with the times. A network of highways linking all parts of the kingdom is part of an efficient, integrated transport system. Thailand's international and domestic air services are first class. There are superb hotels, and government services are moderately better than average for a developing country.

Thailand's value as a business venue is enhanced by its location on major air routes. Bangkok is linked by international airlines to every major city in the world. Adjacent to Bangkok International Airport, the Amari Airport hotel is excellent for small, short-stay meetings. Bangkok is well equipped for conventions and exhibitions in its luxury hotels. Most have a special business centre. The Regent Bangkok is considered one of the best. Services include typing, translating, word processing, copying, dictating, cable, telex and fax. Staff are multi-lingual. Other services include arranging and confirmation of appointments, from 10 baht a call. Pattaya is Thailand's second most important meeting and conference centre. The Royal Cliff Beach Resort is ideal for large conferences and can handle up to 2,000 people. Ancillary services include two elephants bearing the company

BACKGROUND

name to welcome guests and a girl in costume showering flower petals. It is cheap by European standards: from 2,600 baht. The well equipped Regent Cha-Am Beach, in Cha-Am, is another coastal convention site. In Chiang Mai, the Rincome and Chiang Mai Orchid hotels both offer convention and exhibition facilities.

The opening in 1991 of the World Trade Centre in Bangkok has added to Thailand's prestige as a trade and business centre. There are a score of urban conglomerations in Thailand but Bangkok is the only metropolis. Extending more than 618 square miles (1,600 sq km) on either side of the Chao Phraya river, it has a population of 5.6 million (of which 65 per cent is of Chinese descent). The majority of domestic and foreign corporations are sited in the capital.

The hub of commerce and communications, Bangkok is the only place with any degree of western-style sophistication. People working in its high-rise office blocks and shopping complexes perform the same functions as their counterparts in Europe or America. But home life is traditionally Thai.

The product of timeless traditions, country life is in harmony with the seasons. Most farms have been in one family for generations. Common rural settlements line busy roads or waterways. Others are concealed in shady growth in fields. The focal point of every settlement is the *wat,* whose state of repair indicates whether the farmers have enjoyed a good, or a bad season. Most farmers just manage to support themselves. A typical farmhouse is a simple affair, often only a single room which serves for everything, elevated on stilts under a thatched roof. Most farms keep chickens, pigs and a water buffalo used for ploughing.

The family's close communal lifestyle, often including a grandparent, affords no privacy. Children learn to respect their elders from very young. Consisting of anything from 50–150 households, villages are like extended family units. Children call close neighbours 'uncle' or 'aunt', a custom maintained throughout their life. While school is compulsory, they have set chores like penning the ducks and helping at harvest-time.

Life is quieter in the monsoon season. The men may repair their kites during this time and the women manage a little weaving. Sold in the market, home-made cloth helps augment their meagre income. Weddings and births are eagerly anticipated, funerals likewise are attended by everyone. Buddhist philosophy coupled with basic ignorance allows this older generation of Thai peasants to accept their existence. Poor education, though improving, places Thailand at a disadvantage compared with some other ASEAN countries.

Members of the Association of South East Asian Nations are Thailand, Malaysia, Singapore, Brunei, Indonesia and the Philippines.

BANGKOK

For a glossary, see page 124

Thailand's capital, Bangkok, provokes feelings of love and hatred. It has some of Asia's most fascinating sights, but you must suffer to see them. It is hot, noisy and choked with traffic; most of its canals have been filled in to make roads, and flooding is common. That the Thais live in such chaos underlines their reputation for tolerance. Nearly six million people do, half of them under the age of 30.

One of the endearing aspects about Bangkok is the sudden corner of calm encountered when least expected, usually in temples whose high-walled compounds block the noise. Bangkok is a series of such spiritual pockets and patches of vibrant green amid high-rise office blocks. One such is Lumphini Park, a local venue

One of central Bangkok's lovely pockets of green, Lumphini Park

where joggers slog around a serpentine lagoon. Under the trees middle-aged Chinese perform slow-moving callisthenics.

Bangkok's large Chinese population is well integrated, but there is the usual Chinatown, where the noise, crowds and the number of shops selling clothes, gold and noodles – in that order – are excessive, even by local standards.

Most people find Bangkok bewildering because it has no centre. Strictly speaking, this should be the Lakmuang Shrine, where the city was founded and from where distances are measured. But the Democracy Monument, or the new World Trade Centre could just as easily be the centre. Some might nominate the nightclub district of Patpong Road.

BANGKOK – TEMPLES

Even frequent visitors to Bangkok confess to a certain confusion. Orientation is not helped by the city being a flat as a pancake. Its long, straight roads change their names every 20 blocks, and they may only be written in Thai, a swirling script based on Mon and Khmer. Despite an effort by the Tourism Authority of Thailand (TAT) to promote it as a 'walking city', Bangkok is no place for desultory strolls. The best way to commute is by air-conditioned limousine with reading matter for the traffic-jams.

Allow four days for your stay. You will waste one day trying to get to places, and three days are needed to even scratch the surface of the old riverine town. Records from 1557 show that Bangkok was a checkpoint for vessels sailing up the Chao Phraya to Ayutthaya. When Ayutthaya was destroyed, a new site for the capital was selected downstream at Thonburi but, feeling the west bank exposed to further attack from the Burmese, General Chakri moved his court to the east bank. A Brahmanic pillar sunk in the ground by the river marks the 1782 founding of Bangkok. General Chakri, who took the name Ramatibodi – Rama I – built a new palace compound within the old riverbank fort. The Chinese living amid its ruins were moved to Chinatown and master-craftsmen were deployed to recreate the royal residence at Ayutthaya. The compound contained not only the palace, but the government and judicial offices; and more importantly, Wat Phra Keo. Roughly translated, the 'bang' in Bangkok, Bang Pa-In and other Thai towns means a settlement on water. Bangkok has been a city on water since time immemorial. As recently as the last century, two-thirds of its population lived in floating houses or houses on stilts. The 'Venice of the East' that enchanted Joseph Conrad and other Victorian travellers no longer exists, but river life is basically unchanged. Guests staying in a hotel on the Chao Phraya have an intimate view; taking a boat trip on the river is even better. Heading upstream from the Phra Chao Taksin Bridge you pass eloquent old buildings, once warehouses of the Dutch and French and the British East India Company. The boat rocks in the wakes of rice-barges, water-taxis and stately freighters sailing down to Port Khlong Tuey in the Gulf of Thailand. The rising sun striking riverside temples is one of the great sights of Southeast Asia. Alone, this is worth the trials and tribulations of Bangkok.

Temples of Bangkok

Suggesting monasteries on a sightseeing tour of Bangkok is like telling tourists to visit churches in London. Both are houses of worship, but the Thai *wat* has other functions. One was originally a university, all are treasure-troves of art. People go to another to meditate as well as to enjoy a traditional massage, have their palm read, or to visit a homeopath. A market is held in the cloisters of another.

Effectively there are hundreds of *wats*: you are sure to stumble upon your own favourite. The early morning and late afternoon are the best times for photography.

♦♦♦
THE GRAND PALACE AND WAT PHRA KEO ✓

The Grand Palace complex, with Wat Phra Keo (the Temple of the Emerald Buddha), is the most famous landmark in Bangkok; it is not to be missed. A huge compound on the Chao Phraya river opposite the Ministry of Defence, it is hard to miss anyway. There is no more evocative group of buildings anywhere in the world. Inside is the serene, fairy-tale world of ancient Siam.

Surrounded by high, white walls, the complex was originally built by the first king of Bangkok in 1782. Subsequent monarchs of the Chakri dynasty added their own touches. Rama

V chose Victorian-style architecture for the Chakri Maha Prasad, or royal residence, topping it with a traditional curved Thai roof. A golden urn beneath the towering central spire contains the ashes of the Chakri kings. The palace is only used on state occasions: when ambassadors present their credentials, His Majesty receives them on a spectacular niello throne. (The royal family live in the more modern Chitladda Palace near the Marble Temple.)

The large hall on the right or west side of the former palace is the Dusit Maha Prasad, dating from 1789. Built in classic Thai architecture, its roof ends in a tapering gold spire. The small white marble pavilion outside is the Arpron Phimok Prasad or 'Disrobing Pavilion'. The king

The Grand Palace compound has been added to by every monarch since it was built in the 18th century, and is now a strange mixture of architectural styles

Dazzling Wat Phra Keo is the most memorable of all Thailand's glittering temples

used to alight from his palanquin here to remove his ceremonial hat before proceeding inside. (A replica of the pavilion is reproduced in the lake at Bang Pa-In, near Ayutthaya.)

The royal chapel, **Wat Phra Keo**, stands in the heart of the palace complex. Slightly elevated on a marble terrace, it is surrounded by a plethora of gold *chedis*, elephants and temple dancers, sunlight striking their glittering, glass-encrusted costumes. Even the most garrulous tourist is hushed. Discarding your shoes at the door of the temple, you step into another world.

An imitation of the royal temple at Ayutthaya, Wat Phra Keo was built in 1782 to house the Phra Keo Morakot, or Emerald Buddha. Only 2 feet 6 inches (75cm) high, the image sits in a glass case on a gilded altar richly embellished with parasols, golden orbs and mythical creatures – note the negro guardian – towering 36 feet (11m) above the worshippers, many of whom prostrate themselves. The tiny Buddha image is actually carved from nephrite, or jade. Attributed to craftsmen in Chiang Rai in the 15th century, it is well travelled. The Laotians took it to Luang Prabang, from where it went to

Vientiane for 200 years. The founder of the present Chakri dynasty, General Taksin, brought it to Bangkok.

Among his other religious duties, HM King Bhumiphol is responsible for changing Phra Keo's costumes three times a year. The image wears a golden, diamond-encrusted tunic during the hot season, a gilded robe in the wet season and a heavy gold and inlaid enamel dress for Thailand's so-called cool season.

As you leave the temple, have a close look at the murals on the outer cloisters. Beginning on the left as you walk round, they depict various episodes of the Ramakien. Look for Hanuman, the monkey-god, a central character in *khon* (masked drama). The enchanting, gilded creatures guarding the entrances to the Royal Pantheon are *kinarees*, or mythical bird-women.

Open: daily 08.30–11.30hrs and 13.00–15.30hrs. Admission charge (includes entrance to Wimanmek Palace, see page 22). Photography is forbidden inside Wat Phra Keo. Note the image is only open to public view on certain days of the week.

◆◆◆
WAT PHO ✓

Built by Rama I in the 16th century, Wat Pho, or Wat Chetuphon, or the Temple of the Reclining Buddha, is located on the south side of the Grand Palace complex. It is one of Bangkok's oldest temples, regarded by early kings as the country's first university. Within its 8 acres (3ha) are all the different types of Thai religious architecture.

A large *bot* housing a huge Reclining Buddha takes up the northern end of the enclosure. The huge plaster image is gilded with gold leaf paid for by public donations in bowls along its length. Note the soles of its colossal feet, decorated with mother-of-pearl designs depicting the 108 characteristics of Buddha.

Temple rubbings are sold in the courtyard where stone *chedis* or *prangs* seem to grow like plants. There are nearly 100. The largest are memorials to the first four Ramas. Observe the decorative floral ceramics around their base.

Open: 08.00–17.00hrs, admission charge.

Massage at Wat Pho

At the western end of the compound is a traditional Thai massage school founded during the reign of Rama I. Its methods of kneading the pressure points are efficacious, if rather painful. Unlike the other sort of massage for which Bangkok is known, here you keep your clothes on. Masseurs are both male and female (30 minutes is usually enough for most people). Plaques on the pillars of the massage pavilion are inscribed with different herbal ingredients and balms. In the late afternoon, it is crowded with people seeking treatment for rheumatic and other pains brought on by Thailand's humid climate.

◆◆◆
WAT TRAIMIT

on the edge of Chinatown
Wat Traimit houses another Buddha image, this time seated. Weighing 5.5 tons (5.6 tonnes), it is solid gold and sculpted in graceful Sukhothai style. Its existence was discovered by accident only in 1953: being moved to a new building in the temple compound, it slipped off a crane and the outer stucco cracked revealing its secret. The king in Ayutthaya had ordered the gold Buddha encased in plaster to prevent capture by the Burmese.
Open: 09.00-17.00hrs, admission free.

◆◆
WAT SAKET

Ban Bart Road
A landmark of Bangkok is Wat Saket, the Temple of the Golden

The gilded chedi *atop the man-made Golden Mount dominates Bangkok*

Mount. The city's highest point, it is 254 feet (78m) high, and can be climbed via a steep circular stairway for an excellent view of Bangkok. Built in the reign of Rama I, it contains relics of the Buddha presented to Rama V by Lord Curzon of India.
Open: 08.00–17.30hrs, admission charge.

◆◆
WAT ARUN

Arun Amarin Road, Thonburi
Energetic tourists can also ascend Wat Arun, the Temple of Dawn featured on many brochures. Named after the Indian dawn-god, Aruna, its tall richly-decorated *prang* (spire) dates from the early 19th century. It is built on the site of Wat Chang, the royal palace and temple complex when Thonburi was, briefly, capital of Thailand. It housed Phra Keo before the image was transferred to Bangkok. While undoubtedly masterful, Wat Arun is rather plain up close. The best view is from the river at dusk.
Open: 08.00–17.00hrs, admission charge.

◆◆
WAT RAJANADA

Mahachai Road, near Golden Mount
Wat Rajanada was built by Rama III in the mid-19th century. A palm-lined approach along white-washed walls invokes the feeling of a North African mosque. A market within the compound sells Buddhist amulets and other religious reliquaries. Different Indian and Chinese deities are also sold. Stall 61 has some genuine antiques at sky-high prices. Bargain vigorously.

WAT BENCHAMABOPHIT

Si Ayutthaya Road
Also known as the Marble
Temple, within walking distance
of Wat Rajanada, on the edge of
the green heart of Bangkok.
Finished only in 1911, its Thai-
Renaissance style uses Italian
Carrara marble. Guarded by two
large Chinese lions, cloisters in
the *bot* feature 51 Buddha
images; inside is a bronze
replica of the Buddha image at
Phitsanulok, an old town in
northern Thailand destroyed by
fire in 1960.
The rear courtyard of the *wat*
features an old *Bodhi* tree said to
have been grown from a seed
from Buddha's birthplace in
India. In the early morning
monks wait outside the gate for
food.
Open: 08.00–17.00hrs, admission
charge.

Other Temples

Among Bangkok's hundreds of
other temples, the following are
noteworthy: **Wat Mahathat**, the
Temple of the Great Relic; very
old and famous as a meditation
centre, located on Na Prathat
Road between the universities
(open 09.00–17.00hrs, admission
free). Nineteenth-century **Wat
Suthat**, known for its excellent
murals, is in Bamrung Muang
Road and open from
09.00–17.00hrs, admission free.
Wat Indraviharn, built during
the reign of Rama IV, is noted for
its 105-foot (32m) tall standing
image of the Buddha, the topknot
of which contains a relic. Open
daily, admission free, it can be
found on Witsut Kasat Road in the
Bangkhunphrom district.

Secular Sights in Bangkok

Conducted tours of these places
are recommended: see list of
Bangkok travel agents, page
122.

LAKMUANG SHRINE

*outside the Ministry of Defence,
opposite the Grand Palace
complex*
The Lakmuang Shrine is a
gracious, multi-roofed little
pagoda, built over the
foundation stone of Bangkok
placed there by Rama I in 1782.
While its phallic shape cannot
be explained, its powers are
considered fortuitous.
All day long, especially in the
late afternoon, the shrine is a
hive of activity. On the left side
of the entrance, Thai dancers
are seen performing in a small
pavilion. Ahead is an altar
where people burn incense and
rattle 'lucky sticks'. Other
pilgrims smear gold leaf on
elephant guardians of the
shrine. Hawkers sell cages of
birds to release.
Open: 24 hours, admission free.

ROYAL BARGES

The Royal Barge Museum is
located on Khlong Bangkok Noi,
an upstream tributary of the
Chao Phraya. The cheapest way
to visit it is by long-tail boat from
Tha Chang pier.
The ornate barges were used at
kathin, when the king presented
new robes to the monks in Wat
Arun. Seated on a high throne,
sheltered by an umbrella, he
was rowed down the river by
54 oarsmen with a singer
keeping rhythm. The oldest,
longest, most spectacularly

carved barge is *Sri Supannahong*, its gilded prow sculptured like the head of a *hongsa*, or sacred swan. Annual swan boat races are held on the Chao Phraya.
Open: 08.30hrs–16.30hrs, admission charge.

◆

WIMANMEK (CELESTIAL PALACE)
behind National Assembly
Built by King Chulalongkorn in 1900, the four-storey mansion is the largest teakwood building in the world. Set in peaceful gardens, it was designed by Prince Naris, a famous architect of the Rattanakosh period. The royal family was in residence for only two years after which it lay forgotten. Under the patronage of HM Queen Sirikit, it was recently opened to the public. Thirty of the 81 rooms can be seen. The first two contain a treasure-trove of delicate, silver betel-nut boxes. (Offering guests betel-nut to chew is an ancient custom in Thailand.) Other rooms display artefacts, mainly porcelain, bought by King Chulalongkorn abroad. Most of the other furniture is western-style oak and mahogany, the Octagonal Room is one of the most elegant. Blue and white porcelain artefacts are on display in the Chinese Room. A Music Room exhibits traditional instruments of the time. Mounted elephant tusks are a frequent feature. Well lit, rooms in the Wimanmek are cleverly designed and decorated. They are neither so large as to diminish the status of a visitor,

nor so small as to force intimate contact with royalty.
Open: daily 09.30–16.00hrs, admission charge (included in the ticket to the Grand Palace). Guide available. Photography prohibited.

◆

SUAN PAKKARD PALACE
Si Ayutthaya Road near Phaya Thai Road intersection
The Suan Pakkard complex comprises five Thai houses in a landscaped garden belonging to Princess Chumbhot of Nagara Svarga. On display are valuable *objets d'art:* Buddha images, Khmer statues, Ban Chiang pottery. The rear pavilion with its decorated black and gold lacquerwork panels was brought from Ayutthaya and reassembled here.
Open: daily, except Sunday, 09.00–16.00hrs. Admission charge.

◆

BAN KAMTHIENG
131 Soi Asok (Soi 21) Sukhumit
Ban Kamthieng is another charming reassembled 200-year-old house, brought from Chiang Mai.
Open: Tuesday to Saturday, 09.00–12.00hrs and 13.00–17.00hrs, admission charge.

◆◆

JIM THOMPSON'S HOUSE
Soi Kasemsan 2, off Rama I Road
Jim Thompson's House is one of those corners of sudden calm. It belonged to an American credited with reviving the local silk industry after the war. A group of seven teak houses, it contains priceless Asian

antiquities: blue and white Ming pottery, five-colour Benjarong porcelain, Khmer stoneware and exquisite Burmese Buddhas. Once used for card games by Rama V, the dining-table remains set, just as he left it. Jim Thompson mysteriously disappeared in Malaysia's Cameron Highlands in 1967. *Open:* Monday to Saturday, 09.00–16.30hrs, admission charge. Volunteer guides explain the collection.

Wimanmek Palace was built by King Chulalongkorn, who set trends for modern-day Thailand

◆◆
NATIONAL MUSEUM AND NATIONAL THEATRE
Na Phra Lan Road
The **National Museum** is one of the largest in Southeast Asia, containing artefacts from the Neolithic Age to the present Chakri dynasty. Allow ample time for Rooms 7 and 8 which cover the Sukhothai style of the 13th–15th centuries, the first purely local style.
The oldest museum buildings date from 1782. The open-sided Sivamokkhaphiman Pavilion, the original audience hall, houses prehistoric art and Ban Chiang earthenware. Murals in the Buddhaisawan, or former royal chapel, depict events in Buddha's life. The chapel also contains the revered Sihing Buddha bronze image, in early Sukhothai style.
Location: next to Thammasat University. *Open:* daily, except Monday and Tuesday, 09.00–12.00hrs and 13.00–16.00. Admission charge. English-language tours are conducted on Wednesday and Thursday, starting from the ticket desk at 09.30hrs.
The **National Theatre** is adjacent to the museum. An eclectic mixture of Thai and Occidental architecture, it stages classic dances, drama

and other performances.
Special exhibitions of Thai
classic dancing are held on the
last Friday of the month at
17.30hrs. Contact the theatre for
details (tel: 2241342, weekdays
08.30–16.30hrs). Sometimes it
is possible to see a students'
classic dance class in the Fine
Arts Department to the rear of
the theatre.

◆

BANGKOK DOLL FACTORY
Soi Ratchataphan (Soi Mo Leng),
off Ratchaprarop Road
Dolls are popular souvenirs of a
visit to Thailand. You can see
them being made here, and
also buy them. The attached
international doll's museum
contains over 700 exhibits.
Open: daily, except Sunday,
08.00–17.00hrs.

Flower lovers are in for a treat in
Bangkok, where there are
permanent flower and plant
markets and orchid farms, as well
as numerous street stalls

◆

SNAKE FARM
Pasteur Institute, corner Henri
Dunant Road and Rama IV Road
Frankly, there are better snake
farms in this world. There are
bottled exhibits in a small
museum and live exhibits in leafy
pits. The best times to visit are
10.30hrs and 14.00hrs, when
snake venom is extracted from
cobras and other poisonous
species.
Open: 08.30–16.30hrs, admission
charge. Clean toilet facilities.

PLANT MARKETS AND ORCHID FARMS
Bangkok has several lovely plant
markets: **Bangrak**: New Road,
between Silom Road and Sathon
Road; **Pak Khlong Talat**: near
Memorial Bridge; **Thewet**: off
Samsen Road, on Khlong
Phadung Krung Kasem bank;
Phahonyothin: opposite
Northern Bus Terminal.
Plants are 20 times cheaper than
in the west, but impractical to
take home. Orchids and bonsai

can be packed.

Orchid-growing is an important export business in Thailand, similar to the Dutch tulip industry. Orchid nurseries or farms may be visited; many are located in Thonburi, while others line the motorway leading to Bangkok International Airport. Two particularly recommended are: Phairot's Orchids (376 Satupradit Road, Yanawa) and CY Orchids (458/1 Sukhumvit Road). As with other directions in Bangkok, ask the hotel concierge to write the address in Thai as well as telling the driver where to go.

◆◆◆
SIGHTSEEING BY WATER ✓

Although most of the canals that criss-crossed 19th-century Bangkok have been filled in, there are several attractive *khlongs* for water-borne sightseeing, as well as the Chao Phraya river. Khlong San Saep is one. You can catch a boat from Soi 63 or 71 in a southern direction towards Prakanong. Eventually you end up in the country. Other trips can be made by river to the port of Klong Tuey and north to Nonthaburi. The best times are 07.00–09.00hrs and at dusk, but as this is local rush hour, boats are crowded with office workers. To rent your own long-tail boat – a noisy craft propelled by a car engine with a long propeller shaft – costs from 200 baht. The following public boats are virtually free by comparison, but they might be crowded.

Bangkok – Nonthaburi River Taxi: departs every 15 minutes from Wat Ratsingkhon Pier,

06.00–18.00hrs. The easiest spot to board is at Tha Chang Pier, one of the busiest wharves on the Chao Phraya, near the Grand Palace compound. Sights *en route* include the Memorial Bridge, Wat Arun and Thammasat University.

Khlong Mon: departs every 30 minutes from Tha Thien Pier behind Wat Pho, 06.30–18.00hrs. Riverbank temples, orchards, orchid farms and enchanting glimpses of local life.

Khlong Bang Waek: departs from the pier by the Memorial Bridge every 15 minutes, 06.00–21.30hrs. Similar riverine attractions.

Khlong Bang Khu Wiang and Khlong Bang Yai: departs Tha Chang Pier every 20 minutes, 06.15–20.00hrs. This trip passes the Royal Barge Museum and the Khu Wiang Floating Market (until 07.00hrs). Old-style wooden houses with spirit houses stuck in the canal can be seen.

Khlong Om: departs every 15 minutes from Phibun Songkram Pier in Nonthaburi, 04.00–21.00hrs. Riverside life including temples, houses and durian plantations.

Chao Phraya Dinner Cruise: A number of companies such as River-Sight-Seeing Ltd (tel: 4374047) offer two to three-hour dinner cruises on the Chao Phraya.

Travel agencies in Bangkok (see pages 122–3) can arrange water tours tailor-made to your requirements.

Accommodation

Bangkok's wide variety of excellent hotel and guesthouse accommodation is scattered around the city, as it has no

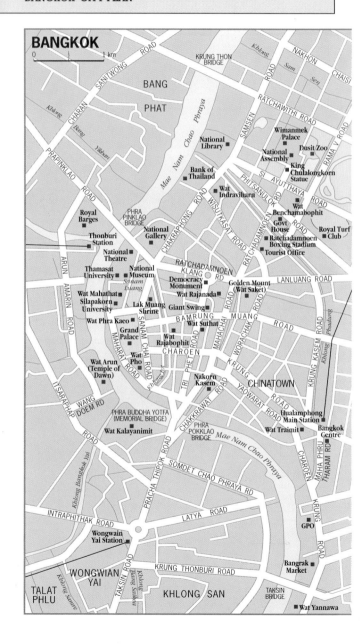

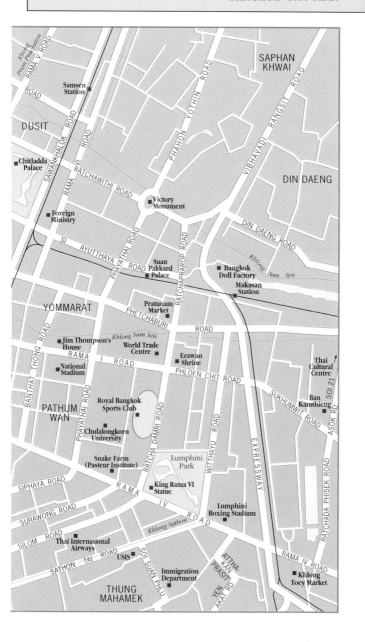

The luxurious Regent Bangkok hotel

centre: the choice of area is up to you. Bookings are essential in the tourist season (October to February). You may like a riverside hotel, in which case there is the world-famous Oriental, the Royal Orchid Sheraton or the Shangri-La. Business people as well as discerning tourists stay at the elegant Regent, handy to the large number of shops at the Ploenchit and Rajadamri intersection, the new World Trade Centre and jogging distance from Lumphini Park. Rooms are spacious, front rooms overlook the Royal Turf Club. Service at the Regent includes a personalised check-in and free local telephone calls.

The Amari Airport is recommended for a final night in Bangkok. Flight advice is posted in the lounge. It is connected by air bridge to the terminal so you can leave 15 minutes prior to check-in (as opposed to over an hour from elsewhere). Several cheap hotels are located in Soi Kasemsan near Jim Thompson's House and Mahboonkrong Shopping Centre. Centrally air-conditioned with a small swimming pool, the Reno is recommended. Cheaper still are the hotels in Chinatown, around Hualamphong and Banglamphu. Backpackers should try guesthouses on Soi Bamphen and Khao San Road.

TAT-listed hotels
The telephone code for Bangkok is 02.

Luxury Class (over B1,200)
Amari Airport, 333 Chert Wudthakas Road, Don Muang (tel: 5661020).
Ambassador, 171 Sukhumvit

Road (tel: 2540444).
Asia, 296 Phyathai Road (tel: 2150808).
Bangkok Palace, 1091/336 New Petchburi Road (tel: 2530510).
Central Plaza, 1695 Phahonyothin Road, Bangkhen (tel: 5411234).
Dusit Thani, 946 Rama IV Road (tel: 2360450).
Hilton International Bangkok, 2 Wireless Road (tel: 2530123).
The Imperial, 6 Wireless Road, Patumwan (tel: 2540023).
Indra Regent, 120-126 Rajprarob Road, Pratunam (tel: 2520111).
Landmark, 138 Sukhumvit Road (tel: 2540404).
Mandarin, 662 Rama IV Road (tel: 2334980).
Manhattan, 13 Sukhumvit Road, Soi 15 (tel: 2550166).
The Menam, 2074 New Road, Yannawa (tel: 2891148).
Le Meridien President, 135/26 Gaysorn Road (tel: 2530444).
Montien, 54 Surawongse Road (tel: 2348060).
Narai, 222 Silom Road (tel: 2370100).
The Oriental, 48 Oriental Avenue (tel: 2360400).
Rama Gardens, 9/9 Vibhavadi-Rangsit Road (tel: 5610022).
The Regent Bangkok, 155 Ratchadamri (tel: 2516127).
Royal Orchid Sheraton, 2 Captain Bush Lane, Siphaya Road (tel: 2345599).
Shangri-La, 89 Soi Wat Suan Plu, New Road, Bangrak (tel: 2367777).
Tara, 18/1 Sukhumvit, Soi 26 (tel: 2592900).
Tawana Ramada, 80 Surawongse Road (tel: 2360361).

First Class (B600–1,200)
Bangkok Centre, 328 Rama IV Road (tel: 2384848).
Century, 9 Rajprarob Road (tel: 2467800).
Continental, 971/16 Phahonyothin Road (tel: 2781385).
Florida, 43 Phyathai Road (tel: 2454552).
Golden Horse, 5/1-2 Damrongrak Road (tel: 2801920).
Impala, 9 Sukhumvit Road Soi 24 (tel: 2590053).
Manohra, 412 Surawongse Road (tel: 2345070).
Nana, 4 Nana Tai, Sukhumvit Road (tel: 2520121).
New Fuji, 299-301 Surawongse Road (tel: 2345364).
New Peninsula, 295/3 Surawongse Road (tel: 2343910).
New Trocadero, 343 Surawongse Road (tel: 2348920).
The Plaza, 178 Surawongse Road (tel: 2351760).
Rajah, 18 Soi 4 Sukhumvit Road (tel: 2525102).
Royal, 2 Rajdamnoen Road (tel: 2229111).
Silom Plaza, 320 Silom Road (tel: 2368441).
Soonvijai Condominium, 1 Soi Soonvijai, New Petchburi Road (tel: 3180987).
Tower Inn, 533 Silom Road, opp Narai Hotel (tel: 2378300).
Victory, 322 Silom Road (tel: 2339060).
Windsor, 8-10 Soi 29 Sukhumvit Road (tel: 2580160).

Tourist Class (B300–600)
Baron, 544 Soi Huay Khwang, Ratchadaphisek Road (tel: 2461520, 2460085).

Comfort Inn, Sukhumvit Road Soi 11 (tel: 2519250).
Crystal, 65 Soi Nathong, Ratchadaphisek Road (near Huay Khwang Intersection), Huay Khwang (tel: 2771012).
Golden Gate, 22/3 Sukhumvit Road, Soi 2 (tel: 2515354).
Grace, 12 Nana Nua, Sukhumvit Road, Soi 3 (tel: 2530651).
In Town, 40/6-7 Sukhumvit Soi 3, opp Bamrungrat Hospital (tel: 2535474).
Ken's Apt and Super Guesthouse, Nana Condo Building, 23/11 opp Rajah Hotel, Sukhumvit Road (tel: 2510218).
Liberty, 215 Pradipat Road (tel: 2710880).

Typical entertainment at the Oriental Hotel: live music and Thai food

Majestic Palace, 97 Rajdamnoen Avenue (tel: 2805610).
Mermaid's Rest, 8 Soi 6/1 Sukhumvit Road (tel: 2533410).
Pradipat, 173/1 Pradipat Road, Sapankwai (tel: 2781470).
Quality Inn, 8/7 Sukhumvit Soi 19 (Soi Wattana) (tel: 2535393, 2527838).
Ra-Jah Palace, 234 Ratchadaphisek Road, Huay Khwang (tel: 2778931).
Ramada, 1169 New Road (tel: 2348971).
Reno, 40 Soi Kasemsan 1, Rama I Road (tel: 215002607).
Rex, 762/1 Sukhumvit Road (tel: 2590106).
Rose, 118 Surawongse Road (tel: 2337695).
Royal Plaza, 30 Nares Road, Bangrak (tel: 2343789).
SV Guest House, 19/35-36 Sukhumvit Road, Soi 19 (tel: 2531747).
Siam, 1777 New Petchburi Road, opp Soi Asoke (tel: 2525081).
Suriwongse, 31/1, 33 Suriwongse Road (tel: 2333223).
Thai, 78 Prachatiphatai Road (tel: 2822831).
Viengtai, 42 Tanee Road, Banglumpoo (tel: 2828119).
555 Wattana Flat, 19 Soi Wattana (19) Sukhumvit Road (tel: 2529697).

Economy Class (under B300)
Atlanta, 78 Soi Sukhumvit Road (tel: 2526068).
Benj Court, 9/28-29 Sukhumvit Road Soi 63 (Ekamai) (tel: 3916669, 3914409).
Chart Guest House, 61 Khao San Road, Banglampoo (tel: 2810803).
Crown, 503 Soi 29 Sukhumvit Road (tel: 2580318).

Freddy's Guest House, 39/7 Soi Ngamduplee, Rama IV Road (tel: 2866722), with branches at 27/40 Soi Sribumphen, Rama IV Road (tel: 2867826) and 34/16 Soi Sribumphen, Rama IV Road (tel: 2871665).

Lee Guest House, 21/38-39 Soi Ngamduplee, (near Malaysia Hotel), Rama IV Road (tel: 2862069).

Montree Guest House, 9/18 Soi Phipat, Silom Road (tel: 2332239).

Niagara, 26 Soi Suksavithaya, Silom Road (tel: 2335783, 2537556).

Prasuri Guest House, 85/1 Soi Prasuri, Dinsor Road (tel: 2801428).

RSC Tourist Guest House, 2/18 Soi Sribunrueng, near Malaysia Hotel .

River View Guest House, 768 Soi Wanit 2, Talad Noi, near River City Shopping Complex (tel: 2358501, 2345429).

Ruamchit Mansion, 1-15 Soi 15 Sukhumvit Road (tel: 2540205).

SD Hostel, 2/27 Phaholyothin Road Soi 40, Bangkhen (tel: 5790110).

Sri Guest House, 1 Soi 38 Sukhumvit Road (tel: 3811309).

Sukhumvit No 1 Guest House, 36 Soi 1 Sukhumvit Road (tel: 2501778).

Sweet House Complex, 5/24 Soi Ngamduplee, near Rama IV Road (tel: 2865774).

YMCA, 27 Sathon Tai Toad (tel: 2872727).

YWCA, 13 Sathon Tai Road (tel: 2861936).

Where to Eat

Highly recommended Thai restaurants in Bangkok include

The Lemon Grass, a palm-shaded, converted Thai house filled with antiques and memorabilia, featuring traditional, especially southern, cuisine; the **Spice Market** (Regent Bangkok Hotel) in an East India Trading Company setting, has dishes graded according to how hot they are, and a daily menu of Thai specialities, the chicken and coconut milk soup being particularly acclaimed; and the **Bussaracum** (Dusit Thani Hotel), with genuine Court Cuisine in a regal setting.

The **Tum Nak Thai** is a must for all visitors: a vast restaurant (seats 3,000) with northern, central and southern dishes brought by waiters (and waitresses) on roller-skates. Tables overlook a lake stocked with gasping carp; there is also a floor-show and surprisingly good food.

These are up-market establishments where a meal for two costs from 500 baht, but there are hundreds of simple Thai restaurants where you can eat well from 60 baht a head. You'll no doubt find your own favourites. Eating at street stalls is safe, anywhere in Thailand. Try those outside River City in Bangkok.

If you don't like Thai food, Bangkok has dozens of different western restaurants, many of which are recommended. Half a dozen Chinese cuisines are also represented, and there are Muslim establishments near the Grace Hotel. The following is a brief guide to dining in the Thai capital:

Thai Restaurants with Thai Classical Dance

The telephone code for Bangkok is 02.

Baan Thai, 7 Sukhumvit Soi 32 (tel: 2585403, 2589517). Nightly from 19.00–22.00hrs.

Kodak Show, Pool Side, Oriental Hotel, 48 Oriental Avenue (tel: 2360400). Every Thursday and Sunday from 11.00–12.00hrs.

Sala Thai, Indra Regent Hotel, Ratchaprarob Road (tel: 2511111). Nightly except Sunday from 19.30–21.30hrs.

Sala Rim Naam, Opposite Oriental Hotel, Charoen Nakhon Road (tel: 4376221, 4373080). Nightly from 19.30–22.00hrs.

Sukhothai, Dusit Thani Hotel, 946 Rama IV Road (tel: 2360450). Nightly from 19.30–22.00hrs.

Tum Tak Thai, 131 Ratchadaphisek Road

It is usually safe to eat from the many stalls selling cooked food in the capital

(tel: 2778833).

Thai Food

Bussaracum, 35 Soi Pipat 2, off Convent Road (tel: 2358915).

Datchanee, 18/2-4 Prachathipatai Road (tel: 2819332).

D'jit Pochana, 62 Sukhumvit Road Soi 20 (tel: 3916401, 3918346). And 1082 Phahonyothin Road (tel: 2795000-2).

Khanom Buang Sukhothai, Sukhothai Soi 4 (tel: 2813496).

Khun Ying, 55 Sukhumvit Soi 63 (tel: 3915769).

Kruathai, Malaysia Hotel, 54 Soi Ngam Duplee, Rama IV Road (tel: 2863582).

Lemon Grass, 5/1 Sukhumvit 24 (tel: 2588637).

Samae San, 65 Sukhumvit Soi 31 (tel: 2584582).

Spice Market, The Regent Bangkok Hotel, 155 Rajdamri Road (tel: 2516127).

Ton Tum Rub, 15-17 Sukhumvit Soi 8 (tel: 2535154).

Ton Khroeng, 299 Soi Thong Lor, Sukhumvit (tel: 3918703).
Wang Kaeo, 74-74/1 Ratchadaphisek Road (tel: 2459134).

Thai and Chinese Restaurants
Ban Bung, 32/10 Ratchadaphisek Road (tel: 2777563, 2778609).
Bangkok Maxim, 62/3-4 Ratchadamri Road (tel: 2526310, 2526334).
Bua Tong, Ratchadaphisek Road (tel: 2455545, 2462159).
Chanphen Restaurant, 1031/1 Rama IV Road (tel: 2860933).
Chao Khun, 68 Ratchadaphisek Road (tel: 2462145, 2462147).
Chao Phraya Restaurant, Pin Klao Bridge, Arun Amarin Road (tel: 4242389).
Chiu Chau, Ambassador Hotel, 8 Soi 11 Sukhumvit Road (tel: 2540444).
Coca, 416 Henri Dunant Road (tel: 2516337).
Downtown, 20 Soi Chidlom (tel: 2521859). And 430/6-10 Siam Square (tel: 2520237).
Dynasty, Central Plaza Hotel, 1695 Phahonyothin Road (tel: 5411234).
Fu Lu Su, 23 Ratchaprasong Road (tel: 2526526).
Golden Dragon, 108-114 Sukhumvit Road (tel: 2514553).
Grand Shangri-La Restaurant, 58/4 Thaniya Road (tel: 2342045).
Hoi Thien Lao, 308 Sua Pa Road (tel: 2211685, 2227191).
Honey Restaurant, 424 Surawongse Road (tel: 2349968).
Jade Garden, Montien Hotel, 54 Surawongse Road (tel: 2348060).
Khum Luang, Ratchadaphisek Road (tel: 2463272).
Maria, Ratchadamnoen Klang Avenue (tel: 2215211).
Mary, 414/5-7 Henri Dunant Road

(tel: 2516802).
Ming Palace, Indra Regent Hotel, Ratchaprarop Road (tel: 2511111).
New Rincome, 144 Silom Road (tel: 2352781).
Rose La Moon, 165/5-6 Sukhumvit Soi 21 (tel: 3917351).
Ruen Phae, 622/103 Charansanitwong Road (tel: 4247563).
Si Fa, 434 Siam Square (tel: 2515517). 47/19-22 Ratchadamri Road (tel: 2537806). 924/31 Rama IV Road (tel: 2353290).
Si Thaiderm, 192 Lumphini Park (tel: 2526330, 2524627, 2526987).
Silom Village, 286 Silom Road (tel: 2339447, 2344448).
Sorn Daeng, 78 Ratchadamnoen Klang Avenue (tel: 2243088).
Tab Kaeo, Ratchadaphisek Road (tel: 2462380).
Tien Kong Restaurant, 77 Soi Nana Nua, Sukhumvit Road (tel: 2514881, 2527593).
Vijit Restaurant, 77/2 Ratchadamnoen Klang Avenue (tel: 2816472, 2820958).

Western Food Restaurants
Captain Bush Grill, The Royal Orchid Sheraton Hotel, 2 Captain Bush Lane, Siphya Road (tel: 2345599).
Castillion Garden, Dusit Thani Hotel, 946 Rama IV Road (tel: 2360450).
Fireplace Grill, Le Meridien President Hotel, 135/26 Gaysorn Road (tel: 2537557).
Indra Grill, Indra Regent Hotel, Ratchaprarop Road (tel: 2511111).
Le Cristal, The Regent Bangkok Hotel, 155 Rajdamri Road (tel: 2516127).
La Normandie Grill, Oriental Hotel, 48 Oriental Avenue (tel:

Thousands of bars and clubs all over Bangkok cater to every taste: this is a transvestite show

2360400).
Neil's Tavern, 58/4 Soi Ruam Rudi (tel: 2515644, 2513603).
Siam Grill, Siam Inter-Continental Hotel, 967 Rama I Road, Pratumwan (tel: 2530355-7).

Vegetarian Food
Cafeteria Bangkok Adventist Hospital, 4th Floor, 430 Phitsanulok Road (tel: 2811026, 2811422).
Himali Cha Cha, 1229/11 New Road (tel: 2351569).
Prakhai, New Fuji Hotel, 299-301 Surawongse Road (tel: 2345364).
Whole Earth Restaurant, 93/3 Soi Lang Suan, Ploenchit Road (tel: 2525574).

Nightlife
World-famous for licentious nightlife, Bangkok offers red-hot, buffet-style entertainment.

Appetisers range from family-type Thai classic dancing and boxing to 'the other', which is what most tourists want to see. After dark the Thai capital assumes its official name – Krungthepmahankhirnbowornrattanakosinmahintarayuthaya-mahadilokpopnopparatratcha-thaniburiromudomratchhaniwet-mahasathan – in short, *Krun Thep* 'The City of Angels', though not perhaps what the ancients had in mind.
Beautiful girls, usually from poor northeast villages, are skilled in all sorts of feats. A 'Light Show' means topless dancing and nothing more. Other acts take place upstairs, with peep-holes to warn of police raids. Neither are Thai men left out of providing entertainment. Some of the most gorgeous girls of all are usually *kra-toeys*, or transvestites. A transvestite show at the Calypso is one of Bangkok's most popular

cabarets.

Privately owned roads, Patpongs I, II and III (gay) have the liveliest nightlife: a sea of neon bar-signs and blaring disco music. There is keen competition for custom. Each bar has a gimmick like screening old American movies or live video acts.

An official Swiss survey shows that, at the last count, Bangkok had 97 nightclubs, 119 massage parlours, 248 disguised brothels and 394 discos-cum-restaurants, all providing a similar service. There are also hundreds of 'love hotels'. Most resemble a motel. A client pulls up outside a room, a curtain drops behind his car and payment is made through a grill. Some simply provide a mattress. Up-market places have everything from ceiling mirrors to undulating beds. You get what you pay for – and careless men pay dearly.

Massage parlours and Bangkok go together like gin and tonic. Open from 06.00hrs to midnight, most offer a professional service not remotely resembling the treatment in Wat Pho. A 'body massage' means sex. There is a basic hourly rate, and the amount to tip depends on any 'extra services'.

While Thai men tend to enjoy themselves in large masculine groups, Thai women are not left out. Massage parlours have now opened their doors to them. One of the few such clubs in the world, Chippendale's (next to the Manhattan Hotel), caters exclusively for a female clientele. Inside are well groomed partners to talk to, to dance with and to indulge

milady's whims. Extras by arrangement. Customers are mainly rich, middle-class Thais. As well as the Patpong district between Silom and Surawongse Roads is Soi Cowboy. Equally famous for nocturnal goings-on, it lies between Sukhumvit 21 (Soi Asoke) and Sukhumvit Soi 23. It too has go-go music, live shows and ultra-friendly hostesses. Silom Plaza on Silom Road comprises bars, restaurants and the Freakout Disco. Sarasin Road (opposite Lumphini Park) is a Thai yuppie hang-out. Good jazz plays at the Brown Sugar Club. Businessmen are recommended the elegant Chamois (41 Soi Langsuan, off Ploenchit Road), which is open from 20.00–01.00hrs. Escort agencies abound for male and female companions. Ask your hotel concierge to recommend one, but wherever you go at night, you'll not be alone for long.

Excursions from Bangkok

Using Bangkok as a base is a comfortable way of sightseeing without having to check out of your hotel each day. Of the following short tours from the capital, some can be made in a day; for others, a two or three day excursion is recommended. See page 124 for a short glossary of Thai words.

◆◆◆

THE ROSE GARDEN RESORT

There is more than roses in this beautifully landscaped riverside complex by the Thachin river in Nakhom Pathom, 20 miles (32km) or about an hour's drive from central Bangkok. Devised by a former Bangkok mayor, it has something for everyone,

The Rose Garden Resort covers a large area of beautiful gardens and tourist attractions – and the food is excellent

and although it sounds touristy, it is done with good taste.
You can spend hours wandering in the gardens, over bridges and lakes. The riverside restaurant serving Thai and western-style food is recommended. There is a swimming pool, a bowling alley, facilities for boating and waterskiing on the river, and a model Thai village. At 15.00hrs a Cultural Show lasting an hour and a half depicts Thai culture in a nutshell: dancing, martial arts, a wedding ceremony and rituals when a Buddhist novice is ordained to monkhood. Indoor seating is around a small arena. Photographers will need a flash. There are good souvenir shops. The resort has accommodation for 177 guests and facilities for small conferences. It is near an 18-hole golf course.
Open: daily, 08.00–18.00hrs. Admission charge (extra for the Cultural Show). Local buses go from the Southern Bus Terminal.

◆◆◆
DAMNOEN SADUAK FLOATING MARKET AND NAKHON PATHOM ✓

Of several floating markets in Thailand, the one most frequented by tourists is on Khlong Damnoen Saduak, about two hours drive south of Bangkok. Tours leave early: by noon the *khlong* is empty of craft.
The town of Nakhon Pathom (35 miles or 56km from Bangkok) can be seen en route. Dating from 150BC, it is particularly sacred to the Thais, as Buddhism was first preached in Thailand near this spot. The 413-foot (127m) spire of the huge Phra Pathom *chedi* looms above the trees. Bell-shaped and covered with tangerine-

coloured tiles, it houses the original *chedi* dating from the 6th century, and four *viharns* with images of Buddha. Trees linked with his life are planted around the outer pavilion.

Half a mile (2km) west of the Phra Pathom Chedi is Sanam Chan Palace. The country residence of Rama VI, it is a fanciful complex reminiscent of an English country estate. The small dog statue represents the king's pet, Yaleh, poisoned by staff for his habit of nipping people.

Returning through Nakhon Pathom at lunchtime, eat at the Kittiwan Restaurant in Song Phon Road 61/65, where they serve good Thai food. Hawkers sell fried bananas, chicken and coconuts around the entrance to the *chedi*.

Coach tours travel direct from Nakhon Pathom to the floating market, along route 325. Independent travellers arriving in the town by bus can take a water-taxi from the bus terminal to the market. Or walk, keeping to the right of the *khlong*.

The bridge spanning the *khlong* is the best vantage spot of the market. Some days there may be 50 to 60 boats, each paddled by a woman sheltered by a blue parasol. Filled with fruit and vegetables, the boats drift along as the women buy and sell among themselves and to householders on the banks. The only men in the floating market are a postman and a butcher. Jostling among the other boats are floating restaurant boats, their owners cooking on small, charcoal stoves. An order is passed from boat to boat to a

customer seated on the bank. Covered stalls lining the *khlong* sell handicrafts. Major credit cards are taken by even the most basic stall. If using cash, bargain vigorously.

How to get there: Bangkok travel agents (see pages 122–3) organise coach tours to the floating market combined with the Rose Garden and Nakhon Pathom. It can also be combined with an excursion to and overnight stop in Kanchana Buri.

Air-conditioned buses leave Bangkok Southern Bus Terminal every 30 minutes from 05.00hrs. Trains leave from Hualumpong Station 10 times a day, taking an hour and a half.

◆◆
KANCHANA BURI AND THE RIVER KWAI

One of Thailand's largest provinces, Kanchana Buri is a green, mountainous area abutting on Burma. The town was established by Rama I as the first line of defence against Burmese invasions through the Three Pagodas Pass. During World War II the Japanese used this route to supply their forces in Burma. Over 100,000 Allied prisoners and local coolies were employed building the 'Death Railway'. This and the bridge over the River Kwai of book and film fame are the infamous attractions of Kanchana Buri. Kanchana Buri is 80 miles (129km) west of Bangkok. The journey takes two hours. You can stop *en route* at Nakhon Pathom. On arrival in the town, visit the TAT office for free maps and brochures (in Saeng Chuto

Road, open 08.30–16.30hrs).
Population about 50,000,
Kanchana Buri is a quiet, old
country-type town. Bicycles are
best for exploring the area: cost
20 baht a day. The bridge on the
River Kwai, or Meklang River, is
3 miles (5km) from the town
centre. It was assembled on site
by POWs. Knocked out in Allied
bombing raids, the central
spans were replaced after the
war. Only the curved arches are
original.
One of the first steam
locomotives to run on the
railway is exhibited beside the

*Testimony to the suffering of
thousands of Allied prisoners: neatly
labelled graves near the river in
Kanchanaburi War Cemetery*

small River Kwai station. Food
vendors find it a good trading
spot. Rafts-cum-floating
restaurants under the bridge
provide indifferent meals to
package-groups. Kanchana Buri
is short of restaurants. The Am-
Coffee-House is recommended.
A night market stays open until
21.30hrs, where stalls specialise
in fried grasshoppers.

In and Around Kanchana Buri

- There are two cemeteries.
The biggest is the **Kanchana
Buri War Cemetery** in the
centre of town; 6,982 soldiers
from Britain, Australia and New
Zealand, Holland and the United
States are buried in small plots,
neatly kept by Thai gardeners. It
is a moving place.
- Smaller and quieter, the
Chung Kai War Cemetery is on
the banks of the Kwai, about 30
minutes by boat.
- The **JEATH Museum** (an
acronym representing Japan
and the allied nations) is built to
resemble a POW camp. Its atap-
huts contain poignant
memorabilia of the suffering.
Located in the grounds of Wat
Chai Chumpol, 550 yards
(502m) from the TAT office, the
museum is open 08.30–16.30hrs,
admission charge.
- Other attractions within easy
reach of Kanchana Buri are the
blue sapphire mines at Bor-
Ploy, 31 miles (50km) away. The
Erawan Falls, 45 miles (72km)
north is one of several in the
area. You need good shoes for
walking through the national
park. Take a swimming
costume. The area is best in the
rainy season when the pools are
full. Bus 8170 from Kanchana Buri

bus station leaves every 50 minutes from 07.00–16.00hrs; it takes an hour and a half.

● Sixty miles (100km) west of Kanchana Buri, the **Sai Yok Falls** is in a national park within the Kwae Noi valley. The best way to go is by boat. A round-trip costs about 100 baht per person (10 people to a boat). It takes over two hours to travel upstream to the falls.

● On the way, the river passes the **Cave of Tham Kung**, with its impressive stalactites and stalagmites. Wildlife is occasionally seen on the riverbank. Raft-houses provide overnight accommodation.

Accommodation

While you can see Kanchana Buri in a day trip from Bangkok, it is recommended to spend a night on one of the floating raft-hotels. The surroundings are peaceful after Bangkok. It is also a little cooler. Run by capable Thai women, the Kasem Island Resort can be found on a private island, 1 mile (1.5km) from the town centre. A boat will pick you up and accommodation is in one of the 25 bamboo cottages with bathroom. There are Thai buffet-style meals with some western dishes. You can swim in the river, or a small pool. The hotel raft, seating about 50 people, makes three river trips a day: at 08.00hrs, noon and 14.00hrs. Thai revellers hire such rafts at the weekend.

Kasem Island Resort is recommended, but it is crowded when fully booked. Charming bamboo-raft accommodation is provided for guests at the Kwai Yai Garden Resort, just over a mile (2km) from the River Kwai bridge. Its well made floating cottages have private bathrooms and a verandah. A boat comes by with Thai titbits to eat. There is a restaurant. The fishing is good and you can dive straight off your raft into the river. For reservations contact:

Kasem Island Resort:
Saengchuto Road, Amphoe Muang (tel: 034 511603). Bangkok reservations: (tel: 02 3916672).

Kwai Yai Garden Resort:
123 Mu 2, Thamakarm Village (tel: 034 513611/2). Bangkok reservations: (tel: 02 2376080/1).

How to get there: Trains depart at 08.00hrs and 13.50hrs from Thonburi Station. The journey takes three hours.

Air-conditioned buses leave Bangkok every half hour (05.30–08.00 and 18.00–22.00hrs) every 15 mins (08.00–18.00hrs). A special tourist programme is recommended: by train, on Saturday, Sunday and holidays. Obtain tickets from Bangkok Hualumpong Station; timetable as follows:

06.15hrs: depart Bangkok
07.35hrs: 40-minute stop at Nakhon Pathom
08.15hrs: depart Nakhon Pathom
09.28hrs: 30-minute stop River Kwai bridge
09.58hrs: depart River Kwai bridge
11.30hrs: arrive Nam Tok Station. Mini-bus to Khao Phang waterfall
14.30hrs: depart Nam Tok Station
16.05hrs: 45-minute stop at Kanchana Buri War Cemetery
16.50hrs: depart Kanchana Buri War Cemetery
19.30hrs: arrive in Bangkok.

A city greater than the London or Paris of its time, Ayutthaya was a great mass of temples and palaces, linked by canals

◆◆
AYUTTHAYA

The ancient capital of Thailand, Ayutthaya (47 miles or 76km from Bangkok) reached the height of prosperity in the late 17th and early 18th centuries. Cargoes from China and the east arrived by boat up the Chao Phraya for trans-shipment overland to Europe. Diplomatic missions were even exchanged with France, and the recently restored Roman Catholic cathedral indicates it must have had a considerable western community.

But life did not run smoothly in Ayutthaya. There were frequent invasions from Burma, when classic battles were fought on elephants especially trained in the techniques of war. One of Thailand's heroines is a queen who was killed in such an encounter. Finally, after a long siege, on the night of 7 April 1767, the Burmese put the great city to the torch.

Present-day Ayutthaya (population 52,000) lies at the confluence of the Chao Phraya and another river and is encircled by a broad *khlong*. A water-tour of its ruins and restorations whets the appetite for a closer look, on foot.

● **Wat Phra Mahathat**: dating from 1384 and restored in 1956. Many valuable objects found on the site are housed in the Bangkok National Museum.

● **Wat Phra Sri Sanphet**: the most important temple within the Royal Palace complex. A standing Buddha image covered with gold was set alight by the Burmese, destroying both the image and the temple. Nearby *chedis* enshrine the ashes of Ayutthaya kings.

● **Chedi Phu Khao Thong**: originally built in Burmese Mon style, the temple was remodelled in Ayutthaya style by King Naresuan, in 1584. To celebrate the Buddhist religion's anniversary in 1956, the Thai government topped it with a 2,500-gramme gold ball.

● **Wat Suwan Dararam**: has been beautifully restored and features typical Ayutthaya-style architecture. Still used as a temple, it is located across the lake from Wat Phra Ram.

● **Ancient Palace**: an enormous complex of intricately carved pavilions. The original, dating from the reign of King U-Thong, was destroyed by the Burmese in 1767.

● **Chandrakasem Palace**: built by the 17th monarch of Ayutthaya, this was also destroyed by the Burmese. King Mongkut ordered its reconstruction as a residence for his occasional visits to Ayutthaya. Now a national museum, it is open Wednesday to Sunday, 09.00–16.00hrs, admission charge.

● **Wat Phra Ram**: begun in 1369, it has been twice restored. A gallery of stucco-work *nagas, garudas* and other mythical statues surround a central *prang*. Elephant gates are found at intervals along the old walls.

● **The Elephant Kraal**: this was used for the training of captured elephants in Ayutthaya times. The last capture was in 1903 during the reign of King Chulalongkorn.

Wat Dhamik Raj is an appealing ruin. Local guidebooks of Ayutthaya's heritage cost 15 baht at the National Museum. Or, invest in a good guide.

Bang Pa-In

A charming collection of palaces and pavilions set by the Pa Suk river, about 18 miles (30km) south of Ayutthaya. Thai monarchs used them during the hot season in the 17th–18th centuries, but the buildings seen today date from the later reigns of Rama V and VI. Most feature an eclectic mixture of styles of architecture. Built by King Chulalongkorn, Wat Nivet Thamprawat is, for instance, typically Gothic, but the Phra Thinang Aisawan Thippa-at in the centre of the lake is Thai. The only building open to visitors is the Chinese-style Wehat Chamrun Palace. The *Oriental Queen* river trip visits Bang Pa-In *en route* to Ayutthaya. On a similar voyage many years ago, a king's wife and her child were drowned before horrified oarsmen who were forbidden to touch royalty. *Open*: 08.30–15.30hrs, admission charge.

How to get there:

Road: direct buses leave Bangkok's Northern Bus Terminal every 40 minutes, from 05.00–19.00hrs. the journey takes an hour and is fraught with the anxiety of road trips in Thailand.

Train: departures from Bangkok Station about 20 times daily from 04.30hrs (taking just over an hour).

River: there is no public boat service, but tourists are recommended to try the one-day excursion on the *Oriental Queen* river-boat, which leaves from the pier of the Oriental Hotel at 08.00hrs and includes lunch and return by air-conditioned coach, or vice versa (tel: 02 2360400).

Rice – the universal staple. It is still cultivated as it has always been, using back muscles and hands

◆
LOP BURI: ANCIENT KHMER OUTPOST

One of the old Khmer capitals, Lop Buri lies 95 miles (153km) north of Bangkok. Records show a community dating from the Dvaravati period (6th to 11th centuries), but subsequent Khmer and Thai settlements have erased all traces. The Khmer kings ruled Lavo, as they called Lop Buri, until the 13th century. Many of its buildings display Khmer-style architecture. Some also have a distinctive French influence: King Narai of Ayutthaya, the main monarch associated with Lop Buri, used French architects to construct his summer palace. The Chao Phraya Wichayen, a residence for foreign ambassadors, is also built in Thai-European design. Among the many interesting buildings in Lop Buri are:

● **Lop Buri Palace** (or Phra Narai Rajanive): the best place to begin a tour. Enclosed by massive fortifications, it dominates the centre of Lop Buri. Note the niches in the inside walls which once contained coconut-oil lamps. Passed on the left as you enter are the ruins of King Narai's elephant stables.

The most significant building within the compound is the Dusat Maha Prasat Hall, or royal audience-room. A 17th-century French ambassador, on being received here, presented King Narai with a set of mirrors, similar to those at Versailles. You can see the mirror-holes in the plaster.

● **Chantheon Pisan Pavilion**, or royal residence, was built by King Narai in 1665 in pure Thai-style. It was restored by King Mongkut in 1863. Today it is the Lop Buri National Museum and is open Wednesday to Sunday, 08.30–12.00hrs and 13.00–16.30hrs, admission charge.

● **Phinan Mongkut Pavilion**, also part of the museum, is a three-storey, colonial-style building used as a residence by King Mongkut during renovations to his palace. Some of his personal effects are seen on the top floor.

● **Phra Prang Sam Yot**: a stucco-work, laterite pagoda dating from the 13th century. Typical Lop Buri style, its three *prangs* or spires represent the three Hindu deities Brahman, Vishnu and Shiva. King Narai converted it to a Buddhist shrine in the 17th century, and like many monuments in Thailand, it displays a mixture of the two great religions.

- **San Phra Kahn**: another Brahmanic shrine dedicated to the Hindu goddess of evil (also called the Kala Shrine). Hundreds of tame monkeys help themselves to the offerings of food and fruit left by worshippers.
- **Wat Phra Sri Maha Thart**: a lofty, 12th-century Khmer temple with several *chedis* in its grounds. It is located opposite the railway station.

How to get there: Independent travellers can catch a bus, or a train. Buses leave Bangkok Northern Terminal every 20 minutes from 05.00hrs until 20.20hrs. The journey takes about three hours. Trains leave Bangkok regularly from 04.30hrs until 22.00hrs. Rapid class is recommended. The train takes over two hours. Apart from the usual danger of driving on Thai roads, the road trip is pleasant. Rice-farms and villages are seen *en route*. Tourists staying overnight in Lop Buri have a choice of half-a-dozen hotels. Most sites can be visited on foot. Otherwise take a *samlor*. Conducted coach tours to Lop Buri are arranged through Bangkok travel agents. The all-day tour is rather tiring, but Lop Buri is a quiet, off-the-beaten-track type of place, not so frequented by tourists.

◆
KORAT (NAKHON RATCHASIMA) AND PHI MAI
With a population of 1.5 million, the town of Nakhon Ratchasima, or Korat as it is more commonly known, is the gateway to the northeast and an important trade and communications centre. Consisting of 17 provinces, northeastern Thailand, or Issan, is today a backward, rural area whose roots go back to a Bronze Age community at Bang Chiang 5,000–7,000 years ago. More recently, it was the hub of a Thai-Khmer civilisation, the main attractions at Phi Mai being only 149 miles (240km) from Angkor, in Kampuchea.
Korat itself has little to interest, but several comfortable – if not glamorous – hotels make it a comfortable base. Monuments are the order of the day. A guide will no doubt point out the shrine to Khunying Mo, a local heroine who rallied the women of Korat during a Laotian invasion in 1826. Of mild interest is a temple on the banks of the Lam Tha Khong river which is designed like a Chinese junk and has won several awards. A recreation park known as Silver Lake, with gardens and water slides is a local, rather than a tourist attraction. Shopping for silk is worthwhile.
The most awesome of the many Khmer ruins scattered over northeast Thailand is the site of Phimai, 37 miles (60km) north of Korat, via Highway 2 and Route 206. Built on an artificial island in the River Moun, Phi Mai is the largest example of Khmer architecture outside Kampuchea, and reached the height of its prosperity under the Angkor monarch Jayavarman VII (AD1181–1201). Built of sandstone and laterite, it features some of the tallest *prangs,* or spires, in Thailand, along with Hindu gods and

scenes from daily life under the Khmers carved in stone as delicately as hand embroidered lace. Many lintels have been reassembled in the Fine Arts Department near the bridge. The ruins are closed at 16.30hrs to prevent pilfering. A giant banyan tree, a mile (2km) outside Phi Mai is worth a visit. You must leave Korat early to visit Prasat Phnom Rung, 50 miles (80km) northeast of Korat in Pra Mai District. Historians believe it was an important halfway house between Angkor and Phi Mai in the 11th–12th centuries. You approach it on ascending levels lined with purifying ponds – essential elements in Khmer designs – and stairways flanked with elephant bas-reliefs and guarded by sacred *naga,* or serpent, balustrades. The main spire in particular reflects the geometric precision of Angkor sculpture. During Songkran, in April, rural people walk in procession up the central stairway.

About 12 miles (20km) from Korat (also off Route 2) is a peaceful monastery known as Prasat Hin Wat Phanom Wan, with dark sanctuaries filled with Buddha images. Note the false windows in its stone galleries and zig-zag designs, which are typical of Khmer craftsmen.

How to get there:

Thai Airways: Operate daily (tel: 044 2800070).
Train: daily 20.30–13.21hrs and 21.00–13.51hrs (express).
Bus: depart from Bangkok North East Terminal at regular intervals, 02.00–24.00hrs.

KHAO YAI NATIONAL PARK

The Khao Yai National Park is worth visiting if you have children with you, but you must arrive at a suitable time for game-spotting, or bird-watching. The road trip from Bangkok takes about three to four hours and there is bungalow-style accommodation for an overnight stay. The 837 square mile (2,168 sq km) park encloses rainforest and grassland, two rivers and more than 20 waterfalls. Birdlife is prolific and animals include elephant, leopard, bear, deer and plenty of monkeys. The TAT guide describes Khao Yai as being 'laced with hiking trails', presumably at one's own risk from its wildlife. Reached at the 102 mile (165km) turn-off from Highway 2. If you book in advance there is a train leaving Bangkok's Hualumpong Station at 06.00hrs, returning the same evening. (See also page 90.)

CHA-AM AND HUA HIN: SEASIDE RESORTS NEAR BANGKOK

Cha-Am (107 miles, or 173km from Bangkok) is the first coastal resort on the sunrise side of the Gulf of Thailand. Hua Hin lies 15 miles (25km) further south. Both are pleasant if you have no time to visit more exotic locations such as Ko Samui or the Phi Phi islands. While unsophisticated when compared to Pattaya, both are safe, family resorts. As such, they are crowded at weekends. Cha-Am has a long, clean white beach lined with casuarina trees and simple seafood restaurants. It is one of those places where you eat to the sound of the waves. No

Royalty at Hua Hin

A royal deer-hunting party discovered Hua Hin's virtues in the 1920's. Prince Chakrabongse, a brother of King Rama VI was first to build there, starting a trend among the aristocracy. In 1925, King Rama VII built a summer palace by the beach (about 4 miles, or 6km, from the present town). He called it Klai Kangwon, meaning 'Far from Worry' and was in residence in June 1932 when a bloodless coup replaced the absolute monarchy with a constitutional one. A keen sailor, the present monarch is often seen at the helm of his yacht off Hua Hin.

frills, though. the large Regent Cha-Am Beach (no connection with the Regent Bangkok) has first-class accommodation. The beach-side bungalows are best. Watersports include sailing, windsurfing, jet-ski and speedboat. Swimming in the sea is safe, but watch out for jellyfish. The hotel has a huge swimming-pool. A free coach service operates three times daily to the town of Cha-Am. The direct Diamond Coach from Bangkok departs at 09.00hrs and takes about three hours. Development in both Cha-Am and Hua Hin is prevented by wealthy owners of seaside blocks.

Hua Hin is an important fishing port. Trawlers unload their catch on its long wharf from 06.00hrs. Avoid the fish market as the day heats up. The local beach

The safe and sandy beach at Cha-Am makes it a popular resort with families

extends over 2 miles (4km) to Khao Takiab Hill. On a rented pony you can ride along to the hill where a huge effigy of Buddha looks out to sea. Simple stalls at the base of the hill serve fresh food. Fishing boat hire costs about 600 baht a day. Other activities are sailing, tennis and golf. The 18-hole Royal Hua Hin Golf Course is one of the best in Southeast Asia. Its fairways wind around clumps of tropical vegetation; the higher ones have a view of the gulf.

Train is the best way to travel to Hua Hin, but still takes four and a half hours. You alight at the station and walk across to the Sofitel Centre Hua Hin. Discreet renovations have not spoiled the former Railway Hotel. The old wing in particular retains a pristine, Victorian elegance. Other tourist hotels overlook the

beach. The colourful central market should be visited. If you drive to either resort, Phetcha Buri, 102 miles (165km) from Bangkok, makes an interesting stop *en route*. Short detours can be made to see the hill-top Phra Nakhon Khiri palace built by King Rama IV, and Kaeng Kra Chan reservoir within the National Park of that name. Phetcha Buri is famous for sweets, biscuits and glacé fruits, sold at shops and roadside stalls. *Kanom mor kaeng* is worth trying: it tastes like caramelised coconut.

THE ANCIENT CITY

The Ancient City of Muang Boran is an hour's drive from Bangkok. Try to see it before making a tour of Thailand. Alternatively, go to fill in what you missed. Conceived by a Bangkok millionaire with a great national pride, the Ancient City is a collection of reproductions of Thailand's most significant buildings: ruins, monuments, palaces, temples, even a mosque complete with imam, are set in picturesque gardens. Some models are scale replicas, others are life-size. Great care has been taken to ensure the precise reproduction of the environment in each province. Many buildings that no longer exist are reproduced from ancient records – look for the reconstruction of the Royal Palace and Temple from Ayutthaya. There is a beautiful 'old' teak treasury, built on high stilts to safeguard precious Buddhist scriptures from insects and damp. Refreshments are sold in wooden houses lining a

khlong which even has a miniature floating market. Take bus 25 from Bangkok's Eastern Terminal. *Open:* 08.30–18.00hrs, admission charge.

◆◆
WAT THAM KRABOK (SARABURI PROVINCE)

Wat Tham Krabok is a rather unusual attraction, as it is also a drug rehabilitation centre. Its abbot, Phra Chamroon Parnchand, was a policeman until being ordained as a monk in 1953. With his aunt, he founded Wat Tham Krabok, whose Thai name means 'Temple of the Bamboo Cave', at the base of a soaring rock. Today it houses several hundred drug addicts. You can wander about the temple precincts where addicts follow a tough 10-day cure based on cleansing the system. Treatment centres on taking a herbal medicine whose recipe was devised by the abbot from more than 100 plants.

During the past 20 years, Phra Chamroon claims to have treated 100,000 cases of drug addiction with a 90 per cent success rate. In 1975 he was given the distinguished Ramon Megsaysay Award for services to the community. If he is not too busy, the abbot receives visitors through an interpreter. The monastery grows most of its food requirements. Monks also make and sell their own soap and massage balm.

The road journey to Wat Tham Krabok in Saraburi province, 82 miles (132km) northeast of Bangkok, takes about three hours. Have your hotel pack a picnic.

THE FAR NORTH

Thailand's hill resorts are a haven from the humid south. Many rich southern residents own a second house in the north, as, during March and April, the temperature is several degrees cooler there than Bangkok. The peak tourist period is October until February when the average daily temperature is 77°F (25°C). Nights are cold. September is the wettest month, and trekking is not advisable during the rainy season when many roads become impassable and local tracks are slippery.

Tourists visit northern Thailand for the beautiful scenery and its colourful ethnic hill tribes, numbering about 20. Each has its own customs and costumes, and trekking among the hill villages is a popular activity. Dubbed the 'Rose of the North' in tourist brochures, Chiang Mai is the largest northern town and the second largest town in Thailand. It is still small when compared to Bangkok, however, and unlike the urban sprawl surrounding the capital, you can be in the quiet countryside within minutes from central Chiang Mai. While there is no escaping Thai motorbikes, the atmosphere too is more like that of a large country town.

Northerners enjoy a particular reputation for being warm and hospitable: *mai pen rai* is often repeated in their northern dialect. The gorgeous, light-skinned Chiang Mai women have a habit of winning most of Thailand's beauty contests. Locals – men and women – are also some of the country's most talented artists: painting, sculpting and weaving are a second nature to them. The main activities in the north are agriculture (fruit and vegetables) commerce and lumbering. Tourism and its ancillary trades employ many people.

Hill women making their attractive costumes

◆◆◆
CHIANG MAI ✓

Chiang Mai, about 435 miles (700km) by road north of Bangkok, is most people's first destination in northern Thailand. Its roots go back to the Lanna Kingdom, founded by King Mengrai in the mid-13th century: the present city, surrounded by the moat and wall, dates from 1296. The town changed hands several times, coming under control of Ayutthaya and the Burmese Empire. It was recovered from the Burmese by King Taksin of Thailand in 1774, and has subsequently been a province of Thailand.

Life began again at the beginning of the 19th century, and new hotels and high-rise buildings now herald 20th-century prosperity. Go soon: concrete is gaining ground and there are ominous signs that Chiang Mai will become a metropolis.

A good place to start your exploration of Chiang Mai is the moat around the town which encloses some of its most important *wats* (mostly open 08.00–17.00hrs), admission free. Some temples display Lanna-Thai architecture from the Mengrai period. Note the magnificent wood-carving on the pediments and doors. Those guarded by *nagas,* or long-necked lions, are usually attributed to Pagan. Among 300 ancient *wats* and *chedis* are:

● **Wat Phra Singh**: contains the much travelled, greatly venerated Phra Singha Buddha image. It is supposed to come from Sri Lanka, but the style is Sukhothai. Its head was stolen in 1922. What you see is a replica. The *wat* dates from 1345.

● **Wat Chiang Man**: houses two sacred images of Buddha. One is an 8th-century marble statue, the other is Phra Sak Tang Tamani, the 1,000-year-old Crystal Buddha famous for its rain-making powers. Greatly revered, it is paraded through Chiang Mai on 1 April. The *wat* features vivid murals depicting events in Buddha's life. In the rear of the temple compound is a large, white *chedi* supported by rows of elephants. Wat Chiang Man was built in 1296.

● **Wat Suan Dok**: contains a large, 500-year-old bronze image of Buddha, in Chiangsen style. Murals inside the *bot* feature Buddhist folk-tales. The forest of white *chedis* behind the *bot* contains the ashes of the royal families of Chiang Mai. The tallest is said to enshrine a holy Buddha relic. Wat Suan Dok dates from 1383.

● **Wat Prathat Doi Suthep**: the golden spire on the hill behind Chiang Mai. It is too far to walk (minibuses leave from the Chang Phuak Gate), but thousands of Buddhist pilgrims make the trek each year. Many stories surround the monastery. One relates how a white elephant carrying a Buddha relic was allowed to wander about Chiang Mai. Where it stopped – some say collapsed – at the foot of Doi Suthep, a temple was built. A pagoda covered in gold tiles houses the relic. A cable-car whisks you up to the temple platform for a panoramic view of Chiang Mai. The monastery was completed in 1383.

Also on the Doi Suthep road:

In Wat Chiang Man, a mural of episodes from the life of Buddha

● **Phu Phing Palace**: the Winter Palace of HM King Bhumiphol is 3 miles (5km) from Doi Suthep. Its beautiful gardens are open on Fridays and weekends, 08.30–11.45hrs and 13.00–16.15hrs, when the family is not in residence, usually in January.

● **Meo Tribal Village**: take a left turn about 430 yards (400m) before the palace. You must walk the final distance, about 10 minutes. Older tourists may find it steep. The village is a good example of a traditional hill tribe community. Though commercial, everything is authentic. The Meo here used to grow opium. Today they do well from tourism. You must pay to photograph the tiny women in red-banded, indigo skirts, each a bank of silver jewellery.

● **The Tribal Research Centre**: located on the campus of Chiang Mai University. It has maps, photos, a library and other information for people trekking to the hill tribe villages. The main hill tribes are Meo, Karen, Yao, Lahu, Lesu, H'Tin, Khamu and Marabi. All have Chinese or Tibetan origins. The Karen are the largest group, living mainly on the Thai-Burmese border. They practise crop rotation, from rice to vegetables, and differ from other tribes in having a matrilineal kinship. Marriages are monogamous. The Meo are polygamous animists. Their powerful tribal head, the *shaman,* is a type of doctor-sage. Known for their colourful costume, Meo like to live at altitudes of at least 3,250 feet (1,000m) – significantly, the best height for cultivating opium. Of Tibetan origin, the Lahu are most accessible around Fang. Poorer than most, they practise primitive slash-and-burn cultivation of crops, including opium. Animists, they have distinguishing costumes: men wear a silver breastplate, women are often bare-breasted beneath their open jackets. The Yao come from southern China and grow opium, as well as rice and corn. They write using Chinese characters and are skilled at embroidery. Yao women's costume is the most colourful of all – embroidered jackets and loose-legged trousers with bright magenta scarves worn like turbans. For more detailed information on the hill tribes, visit the Chiang Mai Book Centre or the Suriwong Book Centre. *Research Centre open* daily, except weekends, 08.30–16.30hrs, admission charge.

TAT-listed Accommodation
Chang Puak, 133 Chotana Road (tel: 053 221755).
Chiang Come, 7/35 Suthep Road (tel: 053 211020).
Chiang Dao Hill Resort, 28 Mu 6, Amphoe Phiang Dao (tel: 053 236995).
Chiang Inn, 100 Chang Khlan Road (tel: 053 235655).
Chiang Mai Hills, 18 Huay Kaew Road (tel: 053 210030).
Chiang Mai Orchid, 100-102 Huay Kaew Road (tel: 053 222099).
Chiang Mai Phucome, 21 Huay Kaew Road (tel: 053 211026).
Chiang Mai President, 226 Vichayanon Road (tel: 053 251025).
Diamond Riverside, 33/10 Charoen Prathet Road (tel: 053 270080).
Dusit Inn, 112 Chang Khlan Road (tel: 053 251033).
Erawan Resort, 30 Mu 2 Tambon Pongyang, Amphoe Mae Rim (tel: 053 251191).
Iyara, 199 Chotana Road (tel: 053 222723).
Krisadadoi Resort, Km 14 Hang Dong-Samoeng Road, Amphoe Hang Dong (tel: 053 248419).
Mae Ping, 153 Sridonchai Road, Chang Khlan (tel: 053 270160).
Mae-Sa Valley, PO Box 5 Mae Rim, Amphoe Mae Rim, Chiang Mai 50180 (tel: 053 297980).
New Asia, 55 Ratchawong Tadmai Road (tel: 053 235288).
Northern Inn, 234/18 Maneenopparat Road (tel: 053 210002).
Novotel Suriwongse, 110 Chang Khlan Road (tel: 053

Intricate and highly-coloured hill tribe weaving is prized by collectors

270051).
Porn Ping Tower, 46-48
Charoen Prathet Road (tel: 053
270099).
Poy Luang, 146 Poy Luang
Square (tel: 053 242633).
Prince, 3 Taiwang Road (tel: 053
236744).
Rincome, 301 Huay Kaew Road
(tel: 053 221044).
Royal Park, 47 Charoenmuang
Road (tel: 053 247549).
Sri Tokyo, 6 Bunruangrit Road
(tel: 053 213899).
Suan Rintr, Km 9, Mae Rim-
Sameng Road, Amphoe Mae
Rim (tel: 053 221483).
The Providence (Little Duck),
99/9 Huay Kaew Road (tel: 053
210014).
Wieng Kaew, 7/9 Huay Kaew
Road (tel: 053 221549).

Dining and Nightlife

Among typical northern dishes
are highly spiced Naem
sausages, mildly curried Khao
Soi noodles, spicy fried catfish
and vegetables in pepper
sauce. A traditional dinner, or
khantoke consists of soup, a
variety of curries, vegetable
ragout and 'sticky rice' eaten off
a low table on the floor.
Entertainment is provided by
hill-tribe dancing. Restaurants in
Chiang Mai also serve a variety
of international cuisines and
there are many cheap street
stalls. Recommended are:.
Aroon (Rai) (northern dishes):
45 Kotchasan Road (tel: 053
236947).
Baan Suan (northern dishes):
51/3 Chiang Mai-Sankampaeng
Road (tel: 053 242116).
Kai Yang (northern-style
dishes): Kotchasan Road.
Nanta Duang Den (seafood):

147/1 Chanklan Road (tel: 053
233335).
Fuang Fah (Thai and western):
Novotel Suriwongswe.
The Riverside (Thai and
western): Charoentrat Road.
Nang Nual Seafood (oriental):
Lamphun Road, South Chiang
Mai.
Lanna Khantoke Dinner
(northern food, hill tribe
dancing): Diamond Riverside
Hotel.
Good, fresh Thai, Vietnamese
and Yunnanese specialities are
served in the night market along
Chaiyaphum Road (within
walking distance of the Dusit
Inn). There are more night food
stalls on Bamrungburi Road,
near Chiang Mai Gate.
Daniel's Bar and Lounge
(British-style food): 6/1 corner
Loikroh and Kotchasan Roads.
Nina's Pub and Restaurant
(British-style food): Nandawan
Arcade.
German Beer Garden (German
food): 48 Charoenprathat Road,
Corner Soi 6.
La Grillade (international food):
Chiang Inn Hotel.
Lek House (international,
specialising in grills): 22
Chaiyaphum Road.
Mermaid's Restaurant
(Scandinavian and Thai): 6/1 Soi
8, off Sukhumvit Road.

Chiang Mai swings quietly after
dark and while less flamboyant
than Bangkok, offers similar
attractions on a smaller scale:
discotheques, bars, massage
parlours and cut-rate Thai
hostesses. For a pleasant
evening in a lovely old
restaurant, The Riverside is
recommended. Start with

The basket village of Hang Dong, 8 miles outside Chiang Mai

cocktails, follow with Thai, or western-style food. Book a verandah table. Live music plays at night. Leading hotels such as the Rincome, Dusit Inn and Chiang Mai Orchid also feature live music.

Shopping and Handicrafts
Chiang Mai is the hub of Thailand's cottage industries. You need only visit an emporium or the Night Bazaar to see the wealth of handicrafts. The main shopping area centres on Tha Phae, Chang Khlan and Witchayanon roads. Tapae Road is also recommended.
The nice thing about local shopping is the handicraft community: you can see the articles being made and the skill that goes into them.

◆◆◆
Wood-carving: superb examples of religious and secular carving are seen on many old buildings. Some say the craft was introduced from Burma. Highly commercial,

wood-carving is found all over Chiang Mai. Subjects range from salad bowls to elephants. Craftsmen work at the Chiang Mai Carving Centre, Rajhiansaen Road, and Singharat Road.

◆◆
Silverware: is made in shops along Wua Lai Road. Patterns feature characters and motifs from Thai folk-tales. While finely embossed, it is doubtful whether pure silver is used; but there are attractive bargains.

◆◆◆
Lacquerware: is made in a village behind Wualai Road, near Wat Nantharam. Originally, it was made from the local lac beetle but today commercial lacquer is used. Coated with several layers, a bamboo object – trays and bowls are popular – is allowed to dry, then painted with colours or gold.

Thai Celadon: a jade-coloured, glazed ceramic, Thai celadon is based on an ancient method from Sukhothai times. Of several factories, Thai Celadon (3.5 miles or 6 km from Chiang Mai) on the Mae Rim Road is well known. Beware of forged antique celadon-ware.
Lace-work: Sarapee Handmade Lace, a shop by the old-city moat, produces delicate hand-made lace.

◆◆
Basketry: South of Chiang Mai, Route 108 leads to Hang Dong, where shops specialise in woven straw, rattan and cane articles – fish-traps, birdcages, baskets, mats and furniture. Prices are ludicrously cheap.

◆◆◆
Umbrellas: are one of Thailand's best known handicrafts. They are made in Bo Sang Village, 5 miles (9km) east of Chiang Mai on the Charoenmuang Road. Decorative rather than practical, they are made from cotton, rice-paper or silk, painted with colourful patterns.

◆◆◆
Silk-weaving: 9 miles (15km) east of Chiang Mai, San Kamphaeng is the centre of the thriving local silk industry. Hundreds of beautiful girls work the looms.

Cotton-weaving: Pa Sang, 22 miles or 36km from Chiang Mai, is the 'cotton village'. Dozens more girls are seen at work. Batiks are also made. Chiang Mai offers excellent bargains in cotton clothes.

Markets
Chiang Mai numbers several street markets, of which the Night Bazaar is the most colourful. The stalls open at about 18.00hrs until midnight along Chang Khlan Road near the junction with Suriwongse Road, which is especially convenient for guests staying at the popular Dusit Inn. All sorts of items are offered for sale from ethnic hill-tribe garments to fake Cartier watches. Hill-tribe artefacts – jewellery, embroidery and clothing – are attractive buys and the price is usually half of that in Bangkok. As usual, you should bargain vigorously for anything that takes your fancy.

TAT-recommended Shops in and Around Chiang Mai
Thai Silk and Cotton
Bua Bhat Panich, 147/4-5 Chang Khlan Road, Chiang Mai.
Nandakwang, 330 Lamphun-Lee Road, Pasarng, Lamphun.
Nandakwang Laicum, 330/1 Lamphun-Lee Road, Pasarng, Lamphun.
Parn Chiang Mai, 180 Tapae Road, Chiang Mai.
Promchana Panich, 78 Chiang Mai-San Kamphaeng Road.
S Shinawatra Thai Silk, 14/4-8 Huaw Kaew Road.
Suvaree, 369 Wang-kwa Road, Lamphun.
Shinawatra Panich, 73 Chiang Mai-San Kamphaeng Road.
Shinawatra Trading, 14/10 Huay Kaew Road.
Surai, 65/52-55 Mu 8, T Suthep.
Jinda Needleworks, 59 Soi Ban

Mai, Chiang Mai-Doi Saket Road, Sansai.

U Piankusol, 60 Mu 10, Chiang Mai-San Kamphaeng Road.

Ceramics

Chiang Mai Sungkalok, 5 km Marker, Chiang Mai-Hod Road.

Kitiroj Ceramics, 5/1 M3 Phrachao Tan Chai-Ton Thongchai, Lampang.

Mengrai Kilns, 31/1 Raj-Utit Road.

Pan-Jiang Ceramic Industry, 192 Behind Veruwon Temple.

Siam Celadon, Kilometer 10.3, San Kamphaeng Road.

Other Handicrafts

Alkemal Kannika Thai Crafts Development Co Ltd, 214-216 Tapae Road.

Chiang Mai Sudalak Co Ltd, 99/9 Chiang Mai-San Kamphaeng Road.

Chiang Mai Treasures Co Ltd, 99/4 Chiang Mai-San Kamphaeng Road.

Hill Tribe Products Promotion Centre, 21/17 Suthep Road, (beside Wat Suan Dok) and 100/51-52 Huay Kaew Road (opposite Chiang Mai University).

Sapakorn Artists, 324 Tapae Road.

Siam Royal Orchid Co Ltd, 94-120 Charoen Muang Road.

Suwan House, 57 Mu 3, Bor-Sang-Doi Saket Road. T Tonpao, San Kamphaeng.

Thai Shop, 106 M3 Chiang Mai-San Kamphaeng Road, Buak Krok Noi.

Thai Tribal Crafts, 208 Bamrung Rat Road.

Thiemnil, 439 Pasarng-Lee Road, Pasarng, Lamphun.

Umbrella Making Centre, 111/2 Bor-Sang-Doi Saket Road.

Wood Carving

Chiang Mai Art, 164/1-4 Rajchiansaen.

Chiang Mai Tasanaporn, 123 Chiang Mai-San Kamphaeng Road.

Hand-painted parasols, usually made of silk or rice-paper

Orchid and Jade Factory, 125 Sri Wichai Road, Doi Suthep.
Prapat, 206 Mu 3, Bor-Sang Village.
Sri-Pra-Orn, 107/9 Bor-Sang, San Kamphaeng.
Vichitrsilp Chiang Mai Handicraft Centre, 54/5-7 Singharaj Road.
Jewellery
PN Precious Stones, 95/4-7 Nimmarnhemin Road.
Silverware
Chiang Mai Silverware, 166 Rajhiansaen Road.
Lanna Thai, 79 Chiang Mai-San Kamphaeng Road.
Siam Silverware, 5 Wualai Road.
Tada Handmade Silver, 12 Huay Kaew Road.
Lacquerware
Boon Lacquerware, 9/4 Mu 7, Chiang Mai-San Kamphaeng Road, San Kamphaeng.
Chiang Mai Handicraft, 145/1 Chiang Mai-San Kamphaeng Road.
Ratana, 185/3 Wualai Road.
Sitthiruang Lacquerware, 2 Soi 5 Ko. Nantaram Road.
Vichaikul Lacquerware 1, 13/2 Wualai Road, Soi 5.
Vichaikul Lacquerware, 108/2 Chiang Mai-Hod Road.
Antiques
Banyen, 86/1-3 Wualai Road.

How to get there:
Bus: Air-conditioned buses leave the Northern Bus Terminal, Phahonyothin Road, Bangkok (tel: 2794484) five times daily from 09.10hrs until 21.30hrs, taking 11 hours.
Train: Depart Bangkok 15.45hrs (Rapid), 18.00hrs (Express). Depart Chiang Mai 15.20hrs (Rapid), 16.50hrs (Express). Journey takes about 14 hours.

Reservation: Tickets of all classes may be purchased up to 30 days in advance at the Advance Booking Office in the Bangkok Railway Station, open 08.30–18.00hrs on weekdays and 08.30–12.00hrs on Saturdays, Sundays and official holidays.
Plane: There are three flights daily from Bangkok. Flight time 55 minutes.

Getting About Chiang Mai: The city is small enough to explore on foot. An urban bus service costs 2 baht (minibus, 5 baht) per ride. *Samlos,* or pedi-cabs, must be bargained for in advance. Bicycle-hire costs from 25 baht a day.

TAT Office: 105/1 Chiang Mai-Lamphun Road (tel: 053 248604).

Exploring north of Chiang Mai

◆◆◆
MAE HONG SON ✓

Mae Hong Son (about 75 miles/120km from Chiang Mai) is a serene hill town near the Burmese border. Shrouded in intrigue, as well as mist, it is a melting-pot of hill-tribe cultures. Its age-old ways are not yet affected by tourism: people keep Mae Hong Son time. A market begins at dawn, and by 08.00hrs it is over and the quaint hill-folk have withdrawn. A few shops sell cheroots, vegetables, woven bags and sarongs, but otherwise the town is half-deserted. By dusk Mae Hong Son is dead. At night only opium smugglers are active. A good view of Mae Hong Son is from Wat Phrathat Doi Khong Mu, a Burmese-style temple. For overnight accommodation, the

Mae Hong Son Resort, 3.5 miles (6km) from town (tel: 053 611406), is recommended. Its bungalows are on the Mae Hong Son river. Very warm clothes are needed from November to February.

How to get there: by bus from Chiang Mai is a gruelling, 7–8 hour journey. Flying is also bumpy; there are two or three daily flights, flight time 30 minutes. Car travellers can visit Doi Inthanon National Park (about 40 miles or 65km from Chiang Mai).

Fang, founded by King Mengrai in the 13th century, lies adjacent to the Burmese border, 77 miles (125km) north of Chiang Mai. The doorway to the 'Golden Triangle', it is a natural conduit for opium smuggling. The Thai government works hard to provide other alternatives to growing opium – a timeless source of income. Tourists pass through Fang to make the river trip between Tha Thon and Chiang Rai, an exciting 5–6 hour journey. Boats leave Tha Thon according to demand: the last, at midday, arrives in Chiang Rai before dark. Do not carry valuables; the armed escort on board is no joke.

Chiang Rai: Nearly 500 miles (804km) north of Bangkok and 113 miles (182km) from Chiang Mai, Chiang Rai is the capital of Thailand's furthest northern province. It used to be the capital of the Lanna kingdom and was later conquered by Burma; in 1786 it became part of Thailand. Today it is known for two main things: tasty lychees and the 'Golden Triangle', in Chiang Saen district. Wat Phra Kaeo – near the

hospital – is said to be the original home of the Emerald Buddha. With several small comfortable hotels, Chiang Rai has become a popular base for hill treks. Bangkok to Chiang Rai by bus takes about 10 hours. Thai Airways operates daily flights, from Bangkok and Chiang Mai. Chiang Rai can also be reached by boat from Chiang Mai (five hours).

Chiang Saen: Thirty miles (48km) from Chiang Rai, this is the last village before the 'Golden Triangle'. It is an enchanting little settlement on the banks of the Mekong which deserves a day of your time. Temples worthwhile visiting are: Wat Pa Sak and Wat Prathat Chom Kitti. A small museum opens daily (except Monday and Tuesday) 09.00–16.00hrs, admission charge. There is pleasant accommodation at the Chiang Saen Guest-House up-stream from the police station at 45 Tambon Wiang. Nearby restaurants serve freshly caught fish. Local shops sell fabric and home-made bags.

The **Golden Triangle**, where the borders of Thailand, Burma and Laos meet, is 5.5 miles (9km) north of Chiang Saen. A motorbike is the best means of sightseeing, or a bike, if you've time: they can be rented from the guesthouse. The actual apex of the triangle is formed by the misty confluence of the Sob Ruak and Mekong rivers at Sob Ruak, 7 miles (11km) from Chiang Saen. As well as opium, cross-border smuggling through the Golden Triangle involves manufactured items such as razor-blades, toothpaste and biros going into Burma, and also Laos, and stolen religious artefacts coming out. Tourism has even reached up here: a huge sign on an arch reads: 'Welcome to the Golden Triangle'. There are regular buses from Chiang Rai (an hour and a half) and a daily VIP bus from Bangkok.

Nan lies in the far north, 200 miles (340km) from Chiang Mai. An old town, with some attractive *wats*, one of the best provincial museums (Wednesday to Sunday 09.00–12.00hrs and 13.00–16.00hrs) and an early-morning market (05.00hrs) sells good rattan-ware. There is accommodation at the Dhevaraj Hotel (tel: 054 710094). From Chiang Rai the roadside mountain scenery is spectacular (five and a half hours by bus). There are flights from Chiang Mai daily, except Tuesday and Thursday.

South of Chiang Mai

Both Lamphun and Lampang can be visited in a day from Chiang Mai. If returning to Bangkok by road, stay overnight in the ancient capital of Sukhothai.

Lamphun (16 miles or 26km from Chiang Mai) is one of Thailand's oldest towns, whose main temple, Wat Prathat Hariphunchai, dates from around 1108. The central *chedi* is 195 feet (60m) high, its summit protected by a nine-tiered golden umbrella. A museum houses Lanna antiquities.
Open: Wednesday–Sunday, 09.00–12.00hrs and 13.00–16.00hrs, admission charge.

Lampang is 57 miles (92km) from Chiang Mai. The main interest here is Wat Phra Kaeo Don Tao, a Burmese-style temple

After a day's work, an elephant appreciates a bath and massage

with an impressive *chedi*. Wat Phrathat Lampang Luang, 12 miles (20km) south of the town, is a very good example of Thai religious architecture, with exquisite interior decoration. Thirty-three miles (54km) east of Lampang, behind Pang La village, is the Elephant Training Centre. There are daily shows between 09.00–12.30hrs, admission charge.

The bus to Lampang from Chiang Mai departs from Chang Puak Gate: alight at Lampang bus station and take a *tuk-tuk* into town. There is also a train from Chiang Mai.

THE FAR NORTH – SOUTH OF CHIANG MAI

SUKHOTHAI–CRADLE OF THAILAND ✓

If you are travelling to Bangkok by road, you can see Lampang and spend a night in Sukhothai – literally meaning 'Dawn of Happiness' – the capital of Thailand for about 120 years. It is rich in magical images, but you are advised to visit the information centre and the museum before making a tour of the sites. Records show the ancient Khmers lived in Sukhothai until being driven out by the northern Thai kingdoms who founded the first Thai capital here in 1238. One of eight Thai monarchs was King Ramkhamhaeng who acceded to the throne in 1278. Striking evidence of life under him is provided by an inscription which reads: '…Sukhothai is good. In the water there are fish, in the fields there is rice. The ruler does not levy a tax on the people. Whoever wants to trade in elephants, so trades. Whoever wants to trade in horses, so trades. Whoever wants to trade in silver and gold, so trades…' Obviously an ancient Utopia, the ruins of Sukhothai's walled city and surroundings cover 7 miles (12km). You can't see them all. so have a guide indicate the most important. Unlike most guides, Thais do not suffer from verbal diarrhoea. Rather a lack of it. Impressively restored, the old

There are a number of interesting ruins spread around Old Sukhothai, 7 miles (12km) outside the new town

city area was declared a National Historic Park on 2 July 1988 when officially opened by HM King Bhumiphol, the longest ever reigning monarch in Thai history. (Park open daily, 06.00–18.00hrs, admission charge for each of the city's five zones.)

Ramkhamhaeng Museum: named after the first king, this is open Wednesday–Sunday, 09.00–12.00hrs and 13.00–16.00hrs. Admission charge. It contains the famous inscription and other local artefacts including the noted famous Sawankalok pottery attributed to Chinese artisans.

Wat Mahathat was the city's main monastery in the 13th century. Its architecture shows both Khmer and Sri Lankan styles which influenced early Sukhothai. Other monuments have Hindu origins in stucco-work animals and gods. A classic Sukhothai work is the walking disciple frieze around the base of Wat Mahathat's central *chedi*. The 'lotus-bud style' is also unique to Sukhothai.

◆◆

Wat Sri Sawai, featuring three spear-blade *prangs* or pagodas, is of Hindu origin, built during the Khmer period.

◆◆

Wat Sra Sri is a beautiful Sukhothai-style shrine reflected in a pond.

◆◆

Wat Trapang Thong and Trapang Ngern: the temples of the Golden and Silver Ponds flanking Wat Mahathat are said to be the original site of the 'Loy Krathong' festival.

Wat Phra Pai Luang, located north of San Luang Gate, is a former Hindu shrine featuring Khmer-style *prangs*. A *chedi* is surrounded by seated Buddhas. Archaeologists believe this may have been the centre of the original Khmer kingdom.

Wat Sri Chum, outside the northwest corner of the city walls, encloses the famous Phra Achana image, or Venerable Buddha. The ceiling of the corridor into the shrine is engraved with passages from the *Jataka*.

Sukhothai's hotels are comfortable, rather than luxurious. Transport within the town is by *tuk-tuk* or bicycle, which can be rented cheaply from the museum.

Excursions from Sukhothai

Two to three hours' drive from Sukhothai, Ban Mae Sot is a rather notorious little place on the Burmese border; if the border ever opens, it will be a major checkpoint on the Trans-Asian Highway. A confusion of short streets and busy stalls, its main activities are in fact gems, gun-running and narcotics. If you deposit your camera with the police, they allow you to walk across the Moei Bridge so that you've been in Burma. On the way to Sukhothai from Chiang Mai you can visit the King Bhumiphol Dam by following the road to Hot. Forming a 119 square mile (308 sq km) lake from the Mae Ping river, it is the seventh largest dam in the world. Boat trips up the Ping are arranged by the Far Eastern

Queen Company in Bangkok: until recently the passengers were mainly Thai. The road journey south provides good views of rural Thailand. Major streams converge at Nakhon Sakhon to form the Chao Phraya. Beyond here you will pass Lop Buri, Ayutthata and, finally, Bangkok. Allowing time to visit the above attractions, the road trip from Chiang Mai takes from three to six days.

Hill Treks

Chiang Mai and nearby towns such as Chiang Rai, Mae Hong Son and Mae Sai are the bases for many hill treks. Trekking here has become almost as popular as it is in Nepal. Everyone does it, from grandmothers to backpackers. Some areas are now 'over-trekked'.

The best plan is to make thorough enquiries before setting out. Check with the travel agent where the trek will go. Double-check the route at the Tribal Research Centre in Chiang Mai (see page 49). Establish how many people will be in your group: six is ideal. Endeavour to see who they are before booking. They might be ghastly. Other things to check are: precisely what is covered by the cost, is return transport included, and does the guide speak the local language?

The best trekking period is November–January, when the opium poppies are in bloom. Sharing an opium pipe with a tribal patriarch is almost *de rigeur* on a hill trek. Leave your valuables with a TAT-recommended establishment in Chiang Mai. Travel light. Thai-style food is available in most areas. There are even out-of-the-way guesthouses if you tire of roughing it.

A popular trek is the Chiang Mai–Mae Sariang–Mae Hong Son–Mae Tang–Chiang Mai circuit. You need to allow six days for this one, more if you make the Chiang Rai river trip. These Chiang Mai companies specialise in trekking tours.

Chiang Mai Honey Tour, 73/4 Chareonprathet Road (tel: 053 234345).

Chiang Mai Nice Travel, 247 Chareonrat Road (tel: 053 241912 Je T'aime Guest House).

July Travel Tour, c/o Novotel Suriwongse, Chang Khlan Road (tel: 053 236733).

Lamthong Tour, 77 Tapae Road (tel: 053 235440).

Mau Tour Services, c/o Chiang Mai President Hotel (tel: 053 235116).

Orchid Tour, Orchid Guest House, 22 Moonmuang Road (tel: 053 210599).

Poppy Tour, Tapae Road (tel: 053 236912).

P Jungle Travel Services, 2/1 Chiang Mai-Lampoon Road (tel: 053 221045).

Singha Tour, 261 Tapae Road (tel: 053 234358).

ST Tour, c/o Montri Hotel, Moonmuang Road (tel: 053 236910).

Summit Tour and Trekking, Thai Chareon Hotel, Tapae Road (tel: 053 233351).

View Travel, (tel: 053 233377).

Youth's Tour c/o Chiang Mai Youth Hostel, Manee Nopparat Road (tel: 053 221180).

Young International Travel, 252 Pra Pokklaw Road (tel: 053 2363115).

Many people along the east coast are employed in producing sea-salt

THE EAST COAST

Beyond Bangkok, Thailand's eastern seaboard extends down the Gulf of Thailand to Trat, on the border with Cambodia (196 miles or 315km). The region is known for rubber and gemstones. Rice-growing, fruit cultivation and fishing are important. Scenically it offers lush forests, waterfalls, long beaches and a score of relatively undeveloped islands. The southern group of coral islands dominated by Ko Chang is a Marine National Park. Except for Pattaya, the coast is not geared to international tourism. The main exit east from Bangkok is the Bang Na-Trat Highway. Most traffic takes this fast, two-lane route of little scenic interest. Visitors with transport should follow the old Sukhumvit Road which runs nearer the sea. It gives glimpses of local life: wooden houses with fishing nets line the *khlong,* people stand by the road selling coconuts, mud-crabs and bags of sea-salt, small aquaculture farms have stalls of dried fish and shrimps. This way takes you past the Crocodile Farm at Samat Prakan (see page 111). The old road joins the Bang Na-Trat Highway just beyond Bang Pakong.

◆
CHON BURI

About 60 miles (100km) from Bangkok, Chon Buri is surrounded by sugar-cane, tapioca and coconut plantations. It is also an important centre for oysters. The town itself has no interest apart from two temples. Behind the main market area, Wat Yai Intharam is the oldest in the province. Wat Dhamma Minitr has a tall image of Buddha in a boat. On a hill outside Chon Buri is Wat Buddhapat, or 'Buddha's Footprint Mountain'.

THE EAST COAST – PATTAYA

◆
ANG SILA

Ang Sila, or 'Stone Basin', 3 miles (5km) from Chon Buri, is named after the chain of rocks surrounding the sea. Also known as the 'Chip-Chip' village, it echoes with the craftsmen's hammers chipping out pestles and mortars. Hundreds are arranged on stalls under the trees, but while cheap and well made, they are too heavy to carry as souvenirs. There is an unusual Sino-Thai monastery on the road south of Ang Sila. The *wat* is in the shape of a ship's hull, and more than 300 monastic cells have similar nautical designs. While the abbot is Thai, many of the residents speak the Chinese Chiu Chow dialect. Some of the older people believe their souls will be taken back to China.

◆
BANG SAEN

Bang Saen (6 miles or 10km from Chon Buri) is a popular Thai family resort. Madness prevails at weekends. Mid-week the beach is deserted, but it seems melancholic, as if it were missing the crowds. There is a large aquarium in the Marine Science Centre. Good seafood restaurants. The central market sells good rattan-ware.

◆
SI RACHA

This village 15 miles (24km) from Chon Buri is famous for its seafood accompanied by hot *nam prik si racha* sauce. Local oysters are also good and prices are much less than in Pattaya. Recommended is the Si Racha Restaurant overlooking the bay. There is a small Sino-Thai temple on the offshore rock at the end of a long jetty. The island of Ko Sichang lies 7 miles (12km) off Si Racha. It is a quiet place inhabited by fishermen, traders and customs officials. At weekends, it is crowded with Thai day-trippers. The swimming is good but be careful of sea-urchins. There is a monastery on the island's central ridge. Bicycle hire is about 100 baht. The Si Racha – Ko Sichang boat service operates from 08.30hrs. Last return journey is at 15.00hrs.

PATTAYA

Pattaya, whose name in Thai means 'southwest wind', is located on the Gulf of Thailand, 91 miles (147km) or two and a half hours' drive from Bangkok or three hours by bus from Bangkok's Eastern Terminal; trains at weekends only. It can be visited from Bangkok, but the majority of tourists stay longer than a day. Barely 20 years ago, Pattaya was a little-known retreat for adventurous foreigners and weekending Thais from Bangkok, with no hotels, a couple of restaurants and a small fishing community. Since then it has burgeoned into a global resort almost equidistant in flying time from Europe, Australia and America. There are now more than 21,000 hotel rooms for package tourists on cheap charter flights. Pattaya may set your teeth on edge with its non-stop traffic chaos and beach-hawkers selling everything from fresh fruit to on-the-spot massage, but there is no denying its

attractions; especially for single men. At times the main beach is not as clean as it could be, but swimming is safe and watersports abound. There is also a good choice of hotels within walking distance, but shop around and bargain for any services.

Sport

Pattaya and surroundings have a remarkable variety of sports with facilities comparable with anywhere in the world.

● **Archery**: Outdoor Range, Nong Nooch Village. Located 11 miles (18km) south, off H3. *Open:* 10.00–18.00, daily.

● **Badminton**: Pattaya Badminton Court Soi 17, Pattaya 1km. Equipment available.

● **Bowling**: Pattaya has four bowling alleys. Recommended is Pattaya Bowl in North Pattaya. Air-conditioned, computer scoring, 20 lanes. *Open:* daily 10.00–14.00hrs (tel: 038 429466).

The charming small resort of Bang Saen is near enough to Bangkok (68 miles or 110km) to be extremely popular at weekends with city-dwelling Thais

● **Fishing**: Panarak Park, *en route* to the Siam Country Club, is a freshwater lake. Equipment available. For game-fishing, enquire at Jenny's bar on Beach Road, or Pattaya Game Fishing Club, 325/34-35 Pattayaland Road 1, South Pattaya (tel: 038 429645).

● **Golf**: There are several courses in the Pattaya area. The Siam Country Club is 20 minutes' drive from the town (tel: 038 428002). Visitors admitted. Driving range 164 yards (150 metres).

● **Jogging**: Pattaya Hash House Harriers meet every Monday, 16.00hrs at the Wild Elephant Bar, Soi Post Office.

● **Parasailing**: Hotels: Royal Cliff Beach Resort, Asia Pattaya, Wong Amat and the Montien.

● **Sailing**: Rates for a Laser,

from 300 baht an hour. Hobie cats from 600 baht an hour. Try Sundowner Sailing Services, Ocean Marina, Jomtien Beach, South Pattaya (tel: 038 423686).

- **Scuba-diving**: Seafari Sport Center, Royal Garden Resort Hotel (tel: 038 428126). Dave's Diver Den, 3/3 Mu 5 Nakula Road, North Pattaya. Basic courses from 1000 baht. Total PADI and NAUI tuition available. Some hotels such as the Dusit Resort, Mermaid's Beach Resort, Nipa Lodge and Ocean View offer free instruction.
- **Snooker**: Pattaya Bowl, North Pattaya. 10 tables. *Open:* daily, 10.00–02.00hrs.
- **Shooting**: Tiffany's, Pattaya Soi II Road, North Pattaya (tel: 038 429642). 19 galleries, air-conditioned. *Open:* 11.00–21.00hrs daily. Wide selection of guns.
- **Tennis**: 20 hotels in Pattaya have tennis courts (variable rates).

- **Windsurfing**: Pattaya has more than 20 windsurfing schools.
- **Water-skiing**: Rates by negotiation.
- **Squash**: Cherry Tree, Siam Country Club Road, located 20 minutes from Pattaya (tel: 038 423686).

TAT-Recommended Accommodation
Luxury and First Class (over 800 Baht)
Asia Pattaya, 352 Cliff Road (tel: 038 428602).
Dusit Resort, 240/2 Beach Road (tel: 038 425611).
Golden Beach, Pattaya 2nd Road (tel: 038 428891).
Island View, 401 Cliff Beach Road (tel: 038 428818).
Montien Pattaya, 369 Mu 9, Pattaya Klang Road (tel: 038

Attractions at the luxury Asia Pattaya Hotel include a private nine-hole golf course and parasailing facilities

428155).
Novotel Tropicana, 45 Beach Road (tel: 038 428645).
Orchid Lodge, 240 Mu 5, Naklua Road (tel: 038 428161).
Pattaya Beach Tower, Beach Road (tel: 038 423101-5).
Pattaya Inn Beach Resort, 380 Soi 2, off Beach Road (tel: 038 428718).
Pattaya Park Beach Resort, 345 Jomtien Beach Road (tel: 038 423000).
Regent Marina, 463/31 Beach Road (tel: 038 428015).
Royal Cliff Beach Resort, 378 Pratamnak Road (tel: 038 421421).
Royal Garden Resort, 218 Beach Road (tel: 038 428126).
Sea View Resorts, 500 Soi 18, Naklua Road (tel: 038 429189).
Siam Bayshore Resort, Beach Road (tel: 038 428678).
Siam Bayview, Beach Road (tel: 038 423871).
Wong Amat, Naklua Road (tel: 038 426999).

Tourist Class
(300-800 Baht)
Best Inn, 420/42 Mu 9, Soi Bu Kaow, Banglamung (tel: 038 422248).
Caesar Palace, 176 Mu 10, Pattaya 2nd Road (tel: 038 428607).
Diamond Beach, 373-8 Beach Road (tel: 038 429885).
Diana Inn, 216/6-9 Pattaya 2nd Road (tel: 038 429675).
Garden Square, 131/8 Mu 5 Naklua Road, Soi 12 (tel: 038 422220).
Holiday Corner, 175/51 Soi Diamon 15 (tel: 038 426072).
Honey Inn, 529/2 Soi 10, Pattaya 2nd Road (tel: 038 421543).
Jomtien Bay View, 192 Mu 10

Jomtien Road (tel: 038 425889).
Jomtien Hill Resort, 384/36 Mu 12 Jomtien Road (tel: 038 422378).
Lex, 284/5 Soi 13, Pattaya 2nd Road (tel: 038 425550).
Lido Beach, 236/7-15 Beach Road (tel: 038 429737).
Marina Inn, Naklua Road (tel: 038 421858, 428134).
Mike Hotel, Mike Department Store Building, 339 Mu 10, Pattaya 2nd Road (tel: 038 422222).
Nong Nooch Orchid Wonderland, Najomtien Road, Sattahip (tel: 038 429321).
Ocean View, 382 Mu 10, Beach Road (tel: 038 428084).
Pattaya Park Beach Resort, 345 Jomtien Road (tel: 038 423000).
Pattaya Resort, No. Pattaya Road (tel: 038 428065).
PK Villa, 595 Mu 10, Beach Road (tel: 038 428462).
Prima Villa, 157/22-23 Naklua Road (tel: 038 429398).
Queen Pattaya, 365/4 Mu 9 Central Pattaya Road (tel: 038 428234).
Romeo Palace, 500/21-22 Mu Naklua Road (tel: 038 429022).
Sea Breeze, 347 Jomtien Beach Road (tel: 038 231056).
S S Pattaya, 194/22-35 Mu 9 Pattaya Klang Road (tel: 038 429938).
Sunshine, 217/1 Mu 10, Soi 8 (tel: 038 429247).
Sunshine Garden, 240/3 Mu 5, Naklua Road (tel: 038 421300).
Weekender, 78/20 Pattaya 2nd Road (tel: 038 428720).
Economy Class
(under 300 Baht)
Bar Norge and Guest House, Soi Yamato (tel: 038 424129).
Cavern Guest House, Soi 6 (Yodsak) (tel: 038 437120).

City View Hotel, So Pattaya Beach Road (tel: 038 429331).
Crystal Garden, Beach Road (tel: 038 428629).
Jenny Hotel, Pattayaland 1 (tel: 038 429645).
Jimmy Mac's, Soi 6 (Yodsak) (tel: 038 425418).
Malibu Guest House, Soi Post Office (tel: 038 428422).
Nipa House, Soi Yamato (tel: 038 425851).
Panda Inn, Royal Cliff Road (tel: 038 422949).
Rainbow, Pattaya 2nd Road (tel: 038 428066 ext RAINBOW).
Royal Night, 362 Mu 9, Soi 5 Beach Road (tel: 038 428038).

Where to Eat

Akamon (Japanese): Pattaya Road, North Pattaya (tel: 038 423727).
Buccaneer Terrace (seafood and steaks): Beach Road, Central Pattaya.
Cherry Tree Pub (English): Siam Country Club Road (tel: 038 422385).
Blue Parrot (Mexican): Pattayaland 2 Road (tel: 038 424885).
Dolf Riks (international, speciality Indonesian): Regent Marina Complex (tel: 038 428269).
Deutscher Biergarten (German): South Pattaya Beach Road.
Brasserie Restaurant (international): 288 M10 Pattaya 2nd Road (tel: 038 424367).
Green Bottle (London-grill type food): Pattaya 2nd Road, Diana Inn (tel: 038 429675).
Hafen Stuble (German): Beach Road, Central Pattaya.
Italia Ristorante (Italian): South Pattaya Road.
Kruatalay (Thai): Pattaya Park Beach Resort, 345 Jomtien Beach

(tel: 038 423000).
La Gritta (Italian): Beach Road, North Pattaya.
Mai Kai Supper Club (Polynesian): Beach Road, North Pattaya.
Narissa (Chinese): Siam Bayview, North Pattaya (tel: 038 423871).
O'Hara (snacks): Regent Marina Complex.
Orient Express (European): Nipa Lodge (tel: 038 428195).
Oslo Restaurant (Scandinavian): 325/14 Pattayaland Soi 2, South Pattaya.
Ruen Thai (Thai): Pattaya 2 Road (tel: 038 425911).
Sala Mekong (Thai): Hotel Tropicana (tel: 038 418566).
Somsak (Thai): Pattaya Road, Soi 4 (tel: 038 428987).
Benjarong Restaurant (Thai): Royal Wing, Royal Cliff Beach Resort (tel: 038 421421).
Savai Swiss (Swiss): Pattaya 2 Road.
Chalet Suisse (Swiss): Sunset Avenue (tel: 038 429255).
Tam Nak Nam (Chinese floating restaurant): Pattaya Central Road (tel: 038 429059).
Talay Thong (Thai): Ocean View Hotel (tel: 038 428084).
Also other restaurants along the beach-front area.

Nightlife

Pattaya has been called everything from the 'Queen of Asia's Nightlife' to 'The Biggest Brothel in Southeast Asia'. How you find it depends on what you seek.
A beach version of Bangkok, it lacks nothing in entertainment. South Pattaya, or 'The Strip' is the liveliest area after dark. Between Beach Road and Pattaya 2 Road

The making of neon signs is a thriving industry in Pattaya

and in connecting *sois* (lanes) is the biggest concentration of cafés, bars, discos and massage parlours.

Open-air bars are lined with stools. Most have 10 to 20 hostesses. Customers are under constant assault by people wanting to sell them flowers, tours and to run them up tailor-made suits.

The Top 20 blares from every bar and shop. Even the 24-hour VD clinic has 'muzak'. Noise reaches a crescendo in the huge 'Palladium' entertainment complex, whose disco-theatre has laser lights and 15,000 watts of music power.

Transvestite shows, always popular, are held nightly at the Alcazar and Tiffany's.

Excursions from Pattaya

Golf Courses: You will pass a number of golf courses *en route* to Pattaya. Located at Tambon Bang Phra near Chon Buri, the 18-hole Bang Phra Golf Course is considered one of the best in Southeast Asia. In beautiful surroundings, it has a motel, a lodge and a swimming-pool and is popular with expatriates and visiting businessmen. Caddies are girls. Green-fees are low. The Royal Cliff Beach Resort has arranged a special package for its guests at the Thailand Country Club (18 holes), while the Asia Pattaya Hotel has a private nine-hole practice course.

◆◆
MINI-SIAM

A 10-minute drive from Pattaya, this is on the left side of the road coming from Bangkok. Open from 07.00–22.00hrs, it features many of Thailand's historic towns on a 1/25th scale. Children feel at home here. Admission charge. Shop and refreshments.

◆
KHAO KHIAO, OPEN ZOO

A variety of species roam over a large area, and there is a large aviary, about 10 miles (17km) off the main road via Bang Phra Golf Course. The Chanta Then waterfall, 4 miles (7km) from the entrance, is the zoo's landmark. Hotel pick-up by mini bus; depart 07.30hrs, return 13.30hrs.

◆◆ NONG NOOCH CULTURAL VILLAGE

nearly 2 miles (3km) off the road to Bang Sare

Morning show at 10.00hrs, afternoon one at 15.00hrs. Show features elephant acts, cockfighting, Thai dancing and boxing. There is a small zoo, orchid farm and two restaurants. You can also see trained monkeys picking coconuts. Accommodation is also available.

◆◆ OFF-SHORE ISLANDS

The islands beckon visitors from

The fishing industry is still important to communities all down the east coast; this is the fish market in Samaesan

mainland Pattaya. Travel agents organise day-trips to the most popular, or you can barter with local fishing-cum-charter boats. Daily sea-charter rates range from 1,500 baht for groups of 10 (low season).

Among the most popular islands are **Ko Lan** and **Ko Sak**. Both are quite developed with several hotels, restaurants and bungalows. Ko Lan has an 18-hole golf course.

Snorkelling is good off the southern tip of Ko Lin, Ko Sak and Ko Phai, reached in another hour's boat-ride. Underwater visibility is good for divers. A day trip to one of the nearer islands for swimming and a seafood lunch is recommended.

Ko Samet is another lovely island known for its powdery, crystalline sand, first grade for the glass industry. A Marine National Park, it has not been spoiled by development. Dagger-shaped and nearly 4 miles (6km) long, the island lies off Rayong province. Local travel agents run daily trips from Pattaya, departing at 08.00hrs by mini-bus and boat from Ban Phe; return about sunset. Independent travellers can spend longer on Ko Samet, as there is bungalow-style accommodation and Sino-Thai meals specialising in seafood, at a quarter of Pattaya's prices. Windsurfing gear may be rented on Ao Phai, or 'Paradise Beach'. Beaching and walking are the main activities. There are some secluded bays for camping, but you must carry fresh water from Na Dang, the main village. Malaria is a risk:

take all precautions, including wearing long sleeve shirts and trousers after sunset.
Boats for Ko Samet depart from Ban Phe at regular intervals during the high season. Departures at other times depend on passengers and cargo.

◆◆
BANG SARE

Tourists wishing to avoid the razzamatazz of Pattaya can stay at Bang Sare, about 40 minutes drive further south (turn off at the 147km post).
Two small streets, a fishing fleet moored at the end of a long jetty and a fine example of a Thai temple are the local sights. The Ruan Talay Restaurant on the jetty serves good seafood, ignore its scruffy appearance. A pleasant place to stay is the Sea Sand Club (tel: 038 435163). Located on the bay just north of the village, it has facilities for windsurfing and fishing. Boats are equipped for deep-sea charter, cost from 2,500 baht a day including rods. Fishing for sailfish and marlin is good in the deep water around Khram, Rin and Man Wichai islands. The Thailand Game Fishing Association headquarters is on the Bang Sare jetty, where there are weigh-in facilities.

◆◆
SAMAESAN

Samaesan is an unspoilt Thai fishing village located off the main highway, about 32 miles (52km) south of Pattaya. Good photos are obtained when the fishing fleet returns to port. The Lam Samaesan Seafood Restaurant offers good views of

activity on the jetties jutting into the turquoise bay.
Island-hopping around Samaesan is still relatively unknown to most visitors in Pattaya. Renting a boat is sometimes difficult as few locals speak English. Enquire in the Lam Samaesan Seafood Restaurant.
The island of Rait lies across the channel from the mainland village, the interest here being a large oyster farm jointly run by Thais and Japanese. Samaesan Island lies on the starboard side of the channel; it has simple bungalow-style accommodation. The water deepens off the southern end of Samaesan around two small rocky islands – Ko Rong Khon and Ko Rong Nang.
Ko Chuang is the second largest island after Samaesan. It has a good white sand beach with clear water for snorkelling. Experienced divers can explore a World War II wreck.
To visit Ko Samaesan only, take a ferry from in front of the seafood restaurant. Departures from 08.00–18.00hrs.

◆
RAYONG

The province of Rayong (115 miles or 185km from Bangkok) is known for fruit, especially durian and *nam pla:* you can't miss the amber-coloured bottles of this sauce. You will certainly smell an odour of fermenting fish. The town of Rayong has little to interest. There is a large image of the reclining Buddha in Wa Pa Pradu. On an island in the river 1.5 miles (2km) south, is the

Phra Chedi Klang Nam. Boat races and other festivities are held in Rayong in November. Rayong is best known for Ban Phe fishing village whose jetties are covered in seafood drying in the hot sun. This is where you catch a boat to Ko Samet (see pages 68-9).

Three miles (5km) from Ban Phe, the Suan Son Pine Park offers shady picnic spots and seafood restaurants: Thai-style, expect nothing special. Seven miles (11km) further south is Suan Wang Kaew, with its pleasant beach-side bungalows. Under local management, offshore Ko Thalu is reputed for diving. Other palm-fringed beaches extend along the coastline to Chanthaburi.

◆◆
CHANTHA BURI

The town of Chantha Buri, about 180 miles (290km) from Bangkok, is a noticeably prosperous gem-mining centre. The motorbike is a sign of local wealth: Chantha Buri suffers from noise pollution. Local travel agents organise visits to the mines. Khao Phloi Waen (The Hill of the Sapphire Ring), near the river mouth, is closest to the town. Visitors may do a little prospecting. You keep what you find. The region is noted for good quality star sapphires. Gems are cut and polished in many local shops. As well as gems, reed-ware products are attractive buys. Tablemats, mats, baskets and lampshades are made privately by a local Vietnamese community. They attend the French-built, 19th-century Our Lady of Conception Cathedral. A fine old building, it is the largest Catholic church in Thailand.

Large rubber, tapioca and fruit plantations surround Chantha Buri. The World Travel Service in Pattaya operates daily tours, including lunch and a visit to the mines. Depart Pattaya 07.00hrs and return 18.00hrs. Independent travellers have a choice of three modest hotels in Chantha Buri.

◆
TRAT

Trat is Thailand's most eastern province, jutting like the tip of a pencil into Cambodia, 196 miles (315km) from Bangkok. The road cuts through a green panorama of rubber plantations and rice fields. The small town of Laem Sing is worth a stop. Vestiges of a brief French colonial influence in this part of the world are a red brick Customs House and small prison.

The town of Trat is undistinguished, with several small hotels. The main attraction in this quiet area is the Chang Isles Marine National Park. Boats to visit the islands can be found at Laem Ngob village, 12 miles (20km) from Trat. Ko Chang is Thailand's third largest island. Wild boar roam its forests and it is known for the beautiful Maiyom Waterfall. At Ko Koot, a 45-minute boat trip from Laem Ngob, an attraction is the Than Sanuk Waterfall. The diving is reported to be good. Take everything you may require if visiting these islands in the eastern gulf.

SOUTHERN THAILAND

The beautiful isthmus extending to Malaysia is Thailand's fastest developing resort area. Places such as Phuket that were once a marathon road journey or sea voyage from Bangkok are now linked by air in about an hour. You can even fly direct to Phuket from Europe.

Away from coastal towns and self-contained tourist complexes you can escape into the under-developed, but not impoverished, tropics. The south is Thailand's most prosperous region after Bangkok. Rubber and coconuts flourish. Tin-mining and fishing are important.

If you've had your fill of culture, head south. Superb beaches and stunning offshore islands await you. The diving is superb and watersports abound. Life is casual and cosmopolitan. In the more popular resorts you will rub shoulders with Germans, Swedes, Italians and French. The cost of living is also much cheaper.

Southern food resembles Malay cooking. Rich curries tempered by coconut milk are typical. More meat is eaten by the south's majority Muslim population.

Among the lush paddy-fields and the rubber plantations, a mosque becomes as common as a *wat*. Influenced by Islam, the culture too seems more Malay than Thai. Travelling into the deep south, Bangkok seems light years away. A small separatist movement is centred in towns near the border. But such things do not intrude on holidays. Give or take an odd bandit attack on long-distance buses, Thailand is one of the world's safer spots to take your well earned holiday. Diving, fishing, swimming or merely lying in the limpid sea off southern Thailand is one stop short of paradise.

The ocean-going people of Phuket, Thailand's largest island, still rely a good deal on fishing; excellent seafood is available all over the island

♦♦♦
KO SAMUI
ARCHIPELAGO ✓

Languishing in the Gulf of Thailand, mid-way down the isthmus, the Ko Samui group of islands is becoming popular. Once the retreat of backpackers, the main island of Ko Samui – *ko* means island – now accessible by air direct from Bangkok, is slowly being

The Temple of the Big Buddha, at the northern end of Ko Samui

transformed into an up-market resort. Thailand's third largest island, Ko Samui has a dozen palm-fringed beaches. The two longest – Chaweng and Lamai – are the most developed. Smaller bays such as Chaeng Mon, Thong Yang and Mae Nam look like picture postcards: clear blue sea, white sand beach, lush green coconut plantations. Beaching is the main activity, or non-activity, on Ko Samui. Chaweng is equipped for windsurfing. Fishing boats can be hired. The lush interior offers pleasant walks.

Ko Samui's population of 35,000 is mainly fishermen, coconut farmers and traders, although many people are now involved with tourism. Enthusiastic tour operators welcome the ferry from mainland Suratthani and catamaran from Bangkok. Accommodation is no problem. A friendly tout knows just the place, with transport supplied. Up-market tourists will like the Imperial Tong Sai Bay (tel: 077 421451) where 56 chalets overlook a private bay. Equally good is the Imperial Samui (tel: 077 421391) on Little Chaweng Beach. It has a spectacular swimming-pool formed from natural rocks. Both properties are owned by the popular Imperial Family group of hotels based in Bangkok. Transfers are arranged by Imperial (Bangkok) to Ko Samui.

The main town on Ko Samui is Na Thon, where there are many cafés and shops geared to backpack travellers, mainly young Australians. As such its nightlife involves a considerable amount of beer-drinking and similar activities; not to everyone's taste maybe, but then Thailand does its best to cater for everyone! Outside Na Thon are quiet villages where you can see the daily routine of unloading fishing boats, repairing nets and harvesting coconuts. Everywhere you go on Ko Samui you will smell roasting coconuts: this and the island's laid-back lifestyle remind one of Polynesia. There are several options to sightseeing on Ko Samui, which has 32 miles (52km) of paved roads. You can take a conducted tour with a travel agent from Na Thon, or explore independently. You can hire jeeps or motorcycles, or if you want to commute, local-style, catch a *song tao* – a small pick-up converted into a bus by benches in the rear. As you whizz around the island, the driver calls out the names of the beaches, so you can't get lost. There are two inland waterfalls. Hin Lat is within walking distance of the port. Take your swimming costume. There are also two temples worth seeing: Hin Ngu at the northern end of the island has a large seated Buddha. Ko Samui is surrounded by some 80 smaller islands (only four inhabited) of which the best known are Ko Pha Ngan and Ko Tao, or Turtle Island, whose inhabitants are fishermen and coconut farmers. Until now Ko Pha Ngan has been only modestly developed; many people prefer its quiet pace of life. Yes, quieter even than Ko Samui; cheaper too. Like Ko Samui used to be, is the general view. A boat leaves from Bo Phut Beach (Ko Samui) at 09.30hrs, taking an hour and a half to Chalok Lam (Ko Pha Ngan), back to Ko Samui at 14.30hrs.

Tour operators in Na Thon run day trips to Ang Thong Marine National Park, 19 miles (30km) northwest of Ko Samui. Depart Na Thon 08.30hrs, return 17.00hrs. There is good snorkelling in a lagoon. Take everything you need. Tours depend on the number of tourists and the weather.

How to get there: It is possible to reach Ko Samui direct from Bangkok; there are daily one-hour flights or a catamaran service taking five hours. Otherwise everyone going to Ko Samui is obliged to transit through the mainland town of Suratthani. The rapid overnight train from Bangkok is recommended: journey time, 12 hours (Get a combined rail/ferry ticket.) Air-conditioned buses leave Bangkok twice daily: journey time, 14 hours. The Wang Thai Hotel (1 Talad Mai Road (tel: 077 283020) is recommended for an overnight stay in Suratthani, a large fishing, ship-building and mining town on the Gulf of Thailand.

There are several ways to travel the final leg to Ko Samui. Best is to catch a bus the 44 miles (70km) to Don Sak pier and join the ferry, which takes an hour and a half. Ferries leave at 09.00hrs and 16.00hrs daily. Children may prefer the fun of the express-boat: this takes from two hours. Departures from Ban Don at 07.30hrs, 12.00hrs and 14.30hrs; last return boat leaves Ko Samui at 15.00hrs.

SURATTHANI

Suratthani (402 miles or 644km
from Bangkok) once formed
part of the Buddhist Srivijayan
Empire which extended over
Java, Malaysia and included
much of Thailand. The town
holds little to interest tourists,
but you can visit a monkey-
training centre *en route* to the
ferry (shows daily
07.00–18.00hrs). Have TAT in
Suratthani check someone is
there.

Near Suratthani is the small
town Chaiya, which some
historians consider was capital

*At the training centre in Suratthani,
it takes a monkey on average four
to five days to learn how to spin a
coconut off its stem*

Picking Coconuts
Not any old monkey can be
trained to pick coconuts. The
smartest are the Ling Nang, a
species like a baboon.
Training starts at three years
old. The two-month course is
held at night, so the monkeys
are not distracted. At one of
the so-called schools along the
road you can see them
learning the tricks of the trade:
spinning coconuts, so they
snap off their stem; picking out
green nuts from brown or ripe
ones; then begging a reward.
When a monkey can climb a
palm and knock down a
coconut, he is ready to start
work. If not, he must start
school again. A workaholic
monkey can pick 500
coconuts a day, compared to a
man's effort of 150–200. In
July, a festival on Ko Samui
determines the fastest monkey
coconut-picker.

of the Srivijaya kingdom, about
1,500 years ago. The restored
chedi at Wat Phra Mahathat is in
Srivijayan style. Wat Phra
Boromathat Chaiya is another
revered shrine. Wat Suanmoke
is a forest monastery. Four miles
(6km) east of Chaiya is
Phumriang village, an arts and
crafts centre.

NAKHON SI THAMMARAT

Nakhon Si Thammarat, 487
miles (780km) south of
Bangkok, is an historic town by
many different names. Marco
Polo called it Lo-Kag, the
Portuguese knew it as Ligor; to
Chinese traders, it was Tung

ma-Ling. Even now no one calls it by its full name meaning 'the glorious city of the dead'. Nakhon was once an important city, but when Sukhothai and, subsequently, Ayutthaya, became powerful, it slowly declined.

The old city wall, 7,250 feet (2,230m) long, encloses a rich repository of temples. Wat Phra Mahathat is in particular revered, the tip of its lofty *chedi* covered with 595 pounds (270kg) of gold. Its base is surrounded by small, guardian-like *stupas*. Inside the temple is a collection of Dvaravati sculpture dating from 6th–13th centuries. A sacred Buddha image is housed in the Buddha Sihing Tower, next to the city hall.

The craft of nielloware is attributed to artisans in Nakhon. Niello is a black alloy: a mixture of silver, copper and lead. Heated, it is inserted in decorative patterns in silver and gold objects: precise work, even a small vase takes weeks to complete. Craftsmen still work at the original Nakhon shop on Chakrapetch Road. Nearby attractions are the Phrom Lok and Ka-Rom waterfalls, 15.5 miles (25km) from town. The district is famous for durians. Recommended hotels are the Thai, near the central market, the Montien and Thaksin.

◆◆
HAT YAI AND SONGKHLA
Nearing the end of the long isthmus are Hat Yai and Songkhla. Most tourists do not go this far south, but these towns are important stops for overland travellers to Malaysia. Located only 31 miles (50km) north of Malaysia, Hat Yai is a brash border town with shops of every description, a rowdy nightlife and attendant hostesses. Malays come for the discos and massage parlours frowned on by their Muslim government. Thais go there for the variety of shopping. Wat Hat Yai Nai houses the world's third largest reclining Buddha 115 feet (35m) long, and 49 feet (15m) high. You can enter its abdomen which is complete with sculpted heart and lungs. The temple is located on Phetkasem Road.

Twelve miles (20km) from Hat Yai are the Ton Nga Chang cascades – take a mini-bus from the market. Taxis leave outside the market for Songkhla, 19 miles (30km) away.

Strung along a peninsula, Songkhla is a charming old fishing port, filled with red, blue and green trawlers. The town has a strong Chinese influence. Old Sino-Portuguese style shop-houses line Nakorn Noak and Nakorn Nai streets. The former governor's palace was a sumptuous Chinese mansion. It has been renovated, and is now a museum with a good collection of pottery retrieved from local wrecks (open Wednesday–Sunday, 09.00–16.00hrs, admission charge). Another museum, in Wat Klang, exhibits early Thai-Chinese porcelain and an ancient marble statue of Buddha. A good view of Songkhla is from the top of Mount Tangkuan, a short but steep climb at the lake end of Vienienchum Road.

A visit to the small island of Ko Yaw is worthwhile. It is renowned for a cottage weaving industry producing *phaa kaw yaw*, good quality cotton textile; every house has a loom. Other islands, Maew and Nu (Cat and Mouse), have pleasant spots for swimming.

Prevailing winds in the monsoon season make swimming unpleasant around Songkhla. The most protected, Samila Beach has several cheap cafés serving good seafood; it can be found beyond the bronze mermaid statue. Nearly 2 miles (3km) south of Samila is a Muslim community with highly decorative fishing boats and a heady smell of drying fish. From here, two roads lead south to Malaysia. Via Sadao goes to Butterworth (Penang) on the west coast. A detour to the serene, provincial town of Satun is suggested. Lying offshore are the unspoiled Langkawi islands, a well kept secret among inveterate globe-trotters. Famed for their good diving, the islands belong to Malaysia. From Hat Yai, Route 4 leads directly south to the border. The less frequented east coast road passes quiet fishing communities.

◆◆
PHUKET AND ENVIRONS

The internationally popular island of Phuket – pronounced 'poo-ket' – lies in the Andaman Sea off the southwest coast of Thailand. Attractive beaches and abundant watersports draw many tourists, but fortunately it is big enough to absorb them. A province in its own right, Phuket is slightly smaller than Corfu and is linked to mainland Thailand by a short bridge. Lush and hilly, it owes its wealth to rubber, tin and tourism. Those harbingers of tourism, the hippies, discovered it in the sixties; regular tourists followed, today the jet-set goes to Phuket. Driving in from Phuket Airport you pass another curious monument to Thai heroines. Sisters, they stand with swords drawn and are credited with leading the defence of Phuket in 1785 against the Burmese. The town of Phuket (population 50,000) lies about 20 minutes' drive inland from the main beach resort of Patong. At first it seems crowded and drab, but a close look reveals many charming shop-houses owned by Chinese who dominate trading. Several white colonial-style buildings remind the visitor of Penang. New quasi-Hellenic architecture appears strange, but is not displeasing. Shopping is fair: fake watches, fake Benetton sportswear, peacock fans and carved elephant statues. You don't go to Phuket to shop. While too big to convey an 'island feeling', Phuket is perfect for relaxing before flying home. Sightseeing concentrates mainly on the beaches. Forget the east coast. It is fringed with mangroves. Lined with palm-trees, the sandy west coast beaches are bathed by the warm, unpolluted Andaman Sea. Patong is the most developed of Phuket's beaches – a long stretch of sand with deckchairs, parasols and

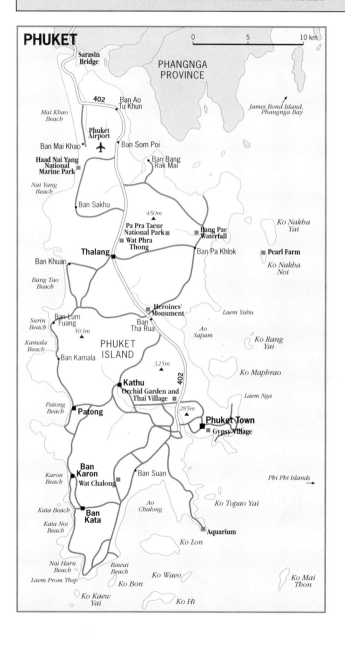

other trappings. Watersports are windsurfing and sailing. Jet-skis have frightened local fish, so deep-sea fishing is an alternative. Sailfish are common victims. You don't have to look for the tour operator; he'll find you. There is less hassle, however, than in Pattaya. Life is pretty easy in Patong, although you might twist an ankle on the walk from beach to shops. The main strip of hotels, restaurants, shops and travel agents runs parallel to the beach. Avoid staying here unless you really like noise: there are motorbikes by day and discos by night. Although small by Pattaya standards, Patong has a lively nightlife. Bars and clubs called Sydney, Paris and the Swiss Garden line Bangla Road. The brightest after-dark district is off Soi Bangla: the same open-arcade bars as Pattaya, full of the same giggling bar-girls.

There are glorious seafood displays outside restaurants in Bangla Road. You will pay dearly to eat here, especially at Restaurant No 4. The cooking is also rough. Try other restaurants on the side street near the Post Office. The uniquely European chef in Phuket is French, employed at the new Meridien Phuket hotel between Patong and Karon beaches.

A pleasant way to visit Phuket's other beach resorts is by motor-scooter, rented from anyone – the waiter, hairdresser, fisherman's brother. Be extra cautious, none is insured and 'Rafferty's rules' apply on the roads. Shared between four, jeeps are good value.

You can no longer find cheap,

Beaches Around Phuket
Mai Khao Beach: lined with familiar causarina trees, and protected during October to February when giant sea-turtles lay their eggs.
Nai Yang Beach: within a national park, near the airport. Good snorkelling on the coral reef.
Surin Beach: isolated, swimming dangerous due to unpredictable undertows. A nine-hole golf course.
Kata and Karon Beaches: neither is as developed as Patong, good diving at the southern end of Kata Noi.
Nai Harn Beach: at the tip of Phuket, this was the hippies' favourite. Today VIPs stay at the Phuket Yacht Club Hotel and Beach Resort here and moor their yachts beneath the cliffs.

nipa-palm huts on Phuket. The majority of accommodation is in air-conditioned hotels and bungalows. Chalet, or bungalow-style accommodation is most appropriate for seaside holidays. The most luxurious complex is the new Amanpuri, which is Indonesian-owned, and high on style and prices, Activities include gym, squash, tennis, windsurfing and waterskiing; a cruiser is available.

The Phuket Island Resort at Rawai Beach is up-market – waterfalls, jacuzzis, package tourists. Club Med is in the usual lovely location at Kata, but once rustic, Kata seems likely to become another Patong. Kata Noi remains on the outside looking in with the 203-room Kata Thani a safe bet.

It is hard to suggest suitable accommodation in Patong. At the south end of the bay, the Coral Beach is isolated, but swimming is poor. Set in huge gardens, the beach-hut style Club Andaman Beach Resort is the best bet. Close enough to walk to town, but out of earshot of its razzamatazz. It is ideal for families.

A worthwhile trip is to the Marine Biological Research Centre, 6 miles (10km) from town. Nakha Noi Pearl Farm, situated on a small island 14 miles (22km) north of Phuket, makes an interesting excursion. Most local pearl farms cultivate only half-orb pearls, but Nakha Noi grows 'proper' ones (daily shows at 11.00hrs, admission charge). If buying pearls, beware of fakes.

How to get there:

Road: Coaches are run by Transportation Co Ltd (tel: 076 4114978-9); Phuket Racha Tour (tel: 076 4121040, 4125944); Suwannachok (tel: 076 4125944, 4126334); Phuket Tour (tel: 076 4121199); Phuket Travel Service (tel: 076 4124847).

Air: Thai Airways operate daily flights to Phuket from Bangkok. Reservations are essential.

Local Transport: In town: Minibus service. From town to the beaches: Mini-buses leave from the market on Ranong Road, every 30 minutes until 18.00hrs. *Tuk-tuk:* Besides local buses,

You need never venture out of the international-standard Le Meridien Phuket on Karon Beach

tourists can also hire *tuk-tuk* to beaches, prices according to the distance. *Tuk-tuk* can be stopped anywhere.

Car Rent: Pure Car Rent opposite Thavorn Hotel; Avis, in leading hotels.

Motorcycle Rent: Motorcycle rental service can be found along Rasada Road and all beaches.

From town to the airport: Local bus leaves daily from the market on Ranong Road from 09.00–10.00hrs. Limousines between Phuket town and the airport correspond to flight times.

Accommodation in Phuket
Amanpuri, Pansea Beach (tel: 076 311394).
Cape Panwa Sheraton, 27 M8, Sakdidej Road (tel: 076 391123).
Club Mediterranee, Kata Beach, PO Box 145 (tel: 076 214830).
Coral Beach, 104 M4, Patong Beach, Kathu (tel: 076 321106).
Dusit Laguna, 390 Srisoonthorn Road, Cherngtalay (tel: 076 311320).
Le Meridien Phuket, 8/5 M1, Karon Beach (tel: 076 321480).
Patong Merlin, 99/2 M4, Patong Beach (tel: 076 321070).
Pearl, 42 Montree Road (tel: 076 211044).
Pearl Village, Nai Yang Beach and National Park, PO Box 93 (tel: 076 311338).
Phuket Island Resort, 73/1 Rasada Road, Rawai Beach (tel: 076 381010).
Phuket Merlin, 158/1 Jarwaraj Road (tel: 076 212866).
Phuket Yacht Club Hotel and Beach Resort, 23/3 Viset Road, Nai Harn Beach (tel: 076 381156).

Not far from fast-developing Krabi, huge slabs of shell fossils jut out into the clear, shallow sea.

PHANG NGA BAY ✓

Phang Nga Bay in the mainland province of Phang Nga is about 47 miles (75km) from Phuket. It is well known for its spectacular scenery – huge limestone cliffs and weird rock formations jut out of the turquoise sea. The bay provided the backdrop for the speedboat chase in *The Man With The Golden Gun*. A road sign before Phang Nga points to the James Bond Island – Khao Phing Kan.

A tour of the bay by long-tail boat costs 500 baht for four hours. Rocks are named after their shapes – Egg, Nail, Puppy and so on. At one point the boat glides over 162 feet (50m) beneath an outcrop known as Tham Lawd. Stalactites encrust the ceiling and, frightened by the noise, bats flap into the light. The shoreline is a tangle of mangroves inhabited by strange creatures like the pig-tailed macaque and walking fish. Outside the entrance to the Phang Nga river is a Muslim fishing village built on stilts. Everything is on stilts, the market, school, even the soccer field. If a ball is kicked over the back line, the goalie must dive into the sea to retrieve it. Accommodation is at the Phang Nga Bay Beach Resort (tel: 076 411067), a comfortable hotel on the riverbank.

KRABI

If you leave Phuket early, Krabi and Phang Nga can be combined in a day. Visit Krabi first and spend the night in Phang Nga. It is only a question of time before Krabi catches up with Phuket. At present its long beaches lined with coconut palms are undeveloped. The most picturesque, Ao Phra Nang, has a comfortable hotel, the Phra Nang Inn (tel: 075 612173). The next beach, Noppharat Thara, is shallow and would suit families. Shell-collecting is good. The particularly ugly Krabi Resort (tel: 075 612160) has accommodation. You go to Krabi to escape the tourists in Phuket, but avoid weekends when it is crowded with local Thais. The food is good and the town on the river has a certain charm, with one or two junks from Malaysia moored at the wharf.

Nearly 4 miles (6km) north of Ao Phra Nang at Susan Hoi is the 'Shell Cemetery', a graveyard of freshwater snails which died some 75 million years ago when the sea flooded inland swamps. The huge slabs are actually billions of shells cemented together by silica deposits. It is one of three such sites in the world. The others are in Japan and America. Refreshments are sold by enterprising Muslims on the hill.

Two attractions on the way to Krabi are Wat Tham Seua, or the Tiger Cave Temple, with dozens of monastic cells built in the limestone cliffs. Older tourists may find the climb arduous. The temple features macabre pictures of cadavers. The Than Bokkarani botanical gardens are a short detour off the road near Ao Luk. Its shady freshwater cascades and pools are ideal for children. Thai families come at weekends when vendors set up their stalls.

SOUTHERN THAILAND – PHI PHI ISLANDS

The sea lake on Phi Phi Lae is formed by a cleft between two limestone cliffs

PHI PHI ISLANDS ✓

Many tourists in Phuket wish they had heard about the Phi Phi (or Pee Pee) islands in advance. Phi Phi Lae and Phi Phi Don are two enchanting tropical islands lying 26 miles (42km) off Krabi province. They are reached by daily excursion boats from either Krabi or Phuket. Departures from Krabi (Chao Fah Pier) are at 09.00, 11.00, 14.30 and 14.40hrs, taking two hours; from Phuket (Thiensin Pier) between 08.30 and 13.30hrs, these are day tours which include lunch and snorkelling. Dumbell-shaped, Phi Phi Don is the larger of the two islands with lush, jungle-clad hills, soaring cliffs and white sand beaches. It resembles the Seychelles. Boats land tourists at Ton Sai Bay for lunch. The Tonsai Village has

bungalow accommodation. Under the same management, the Pee Pee Island Cabana (both, tel: 075 611496) is more up-market. Both face the beach. Day-trippers tend to spoil the atmosphere here, but other places are more remote. Phi Phi Don has a surprising amount of other accommodation, mainly nipa-palm bungalows. Originally fishermen and coconut farmers, many of its 500 residents have turned to tourism. The island is too small to cope with many people, and the high season should be avoided. Although storms are frequent during the low season (June to October), the occasional sunny day is glorious; the average temperature then is 86–91°F (30–33°C). Prices are cheaper by 50 per cent at this time. Backpackers have a huge choice. The small Bay View Resort (tel: 076 214488) with its tiny beach huts, each with toilet and shower, is recommended.

The Pee Pee Village Resort, in a beautiful bay in the northeast coast, has 60 air-conditioned bungalows. The latest development is the 120-room Pee Pee International Resort (tel: 076 214297) near the sea-gypsy village at Tong Cape.

Transport around the island is by long-tail boat: cost (low season) about 150 baht for two hours' sightseeing. Otherwise you walk. There are no cars or motorbikes because there are no roads. The government in Bangkok has forgotten Phi Phi Don. There are no street lights and there is no policeman, but they don't have any trouble. Boats dock at Ao Don Sai, the only village of some 50 houses-cum-shops. People commute along a concrete path by the bay.

At the centre of the village is a huge banyan tree filled with bats: steer clear after dusk. There are two simple restaurants: the Mira Kum (owner unsure of its name), and the Chao Koa, which charges seafood by weight. Both sell Thai beer. Shops have limited Thai-style stock, so take everything you may need, especially mosquito repellent. Phi Phi Don has no nightlife and no watersports. Diving is its main tourist attraction. Coral reefs extend south of Run Tee Bay. Growth starts in shallow water, which is particularly good for beginners. The diving is also excellent off Bamboo island, 50 minutes away by boat. It is a 30-minute crossing from Phi Phi Don to Phi Phi Lae. The

The beautiful white-sand beaches of Phi Phi Don

SOUTHERN THAILAND – PHI PHI ISLANDS

These tiny nests, collected at much risk, are made of the birds' saliva which hardens in the air. When cooked, the nests separate and soften to resemble noodles

smaller island is almost sheer limestone cliffs rising out of the sea. Spectacular turquoise inlets offer wonderful swimming. The best plan is to take a picnic. No one may stay overnight on account of the lucrative birds' nest export business to Hong Kong/China. Tiny – three fit in the palm of a hand – the nests are not twigs and lime as you might think. They are formed from a sticky solution secreted by two glands near the beak of the brown-rumped swift (*Callocalia esculenta*), which nests on Phi Phi Lae. Connoisseurs grade the nests like vintage wine: price $100 per 500 grams. You can see why they are expensive, on visiting Phi Phi Lae.

The birds nest among stalactites jutting off the roof of an awesome cave called the Viking Cave, after early sketches of boats on a wall. The method of amassing the nests is mind-boggling. The collectors, usually Muslim fishermen, must climb long bamboo poles secured only by flimsy raffia. Strapping candles to their heads to light the way, the men ascend hundreds of feet into total darkness. Using long poles, they knock down the nests. Collecting is only permitted twice a year, between March and May and in September, after which the chicks are left undisturbed. A huge stalagmite altar explains the risks involved. Before climbing, the men place white flags and other offerings at its base. Chinese licensees in Phuket pay them 10,000 baht a month. There is no insurance cover. Flashlight photography inside the cave is forbidden.

PEACE AND QUIET
Wildlife and Countryside in Thailand
by Paul Sterry

Thailand is a splendidly varied country. Parts of its extensive coastline would be the envy of any tropical paradise, and it also has coastal plains, tropical rainforests and dramatic mountains to add to the scenic variety. Much of the country was once clad in rainforest or hill forest. Sadly, a lot has now been cleared, and most other habitats have felt some influence from man over the centuries. However, there are 53 national parks covering over 9,652 square miles (25,000 sq km), protecting pristine areas. Thailand is at a geographical crossroad and this is reflected in its wildlife, and in particular in its birds. Many Thai species are widespread on the Indian sub-continent while others are more characteristic of the Australian birds. In addition, Thailand plays host during the winter months to millions of visiting birds from northern Asia.

In and Around Bangkok
Bangkok is within easy reach of many national parks and other areas of wildlife interest, and there is much to offer within the city itself.
The flowering shrubs which adorn the gardens of the capital are the envy of any gardener, as are the orchids: pots of these flowers hang from the walls of almost every house.
Bangkok has no official botanical garden, but the grounds of the Suan Pakkard Palace are well set out. The Lumphini Park in central Bangkok and the Chatuchak Park in the north of the city, although both ornamental, attract a variety of wildlife and provide a good introduction to Thailand's birdlife. Common mynas and black kites are common and brown fly-catchers winter here. Bangkok lies within easy reach of the coast of the Gulf of Thailand. One of the best spots for the visiting birdwatcher is Bangpoo, 15 miles (25km) east of the city. It is an area of saltpans, pools, mangrove and mudflats which attracts large numbers of waders in autumn and winter. The best time to see the birds is on a rising tide when they are pushed close to the shore, and at high tide many visit the pools and marshes to roost and feed. Greater and lesser sandplovers,

A Bangkok garden, with flowering flame tree and coconut palm

PEACE AND QUIET

stints, sandpipers and brown-headed gulls are common at Bangpoo and there is always a chance of a rarity like Nordmann's greenshank turning up. Mangroves' amazing root systems are an endless source of fascination. The branches provide perches for pied and white-collared kingfishers, and flyeaters forage among the leaves. This brown and yellow warbler is constantly active and even sings its wheezing song throughout the heat of the day.

Fruit Bats
Flying foxes, or fruit bats, are probably the most conspicuous wildlife residents of Bangkok and the surrounding countryside. These large bats hang in trees during the day, leaving at dusk in their thousands to go in search of nectar and ripe fruit. Their travels can take them up to 50 miles (80km) from the daytime roost, and they are important agents of pollination and seed dispersal among tropical trees.

Steer clear of large trees in Bangkok around dusk: that's when fruit bats leave them in droves to go hunting

Forests
Although there is considerable variation within the country, most of Thailand's pristine forests fall into the broad category of 'rainforests'. There are only three major areas of rainforest in the world – South America, Africa and Southeast Asia – so Thailand's remaining forests are of global significance.
Rainforests are characterised and maintained by three important environmental factors: constant high temperatures, high humidity and high rainfall. Although rainforests in the three major regions all look superficially similar, the species of plants and animals they harbour could not be more different.
Primary rainforests have a high, dense tree canopy which lets only minimal amounts of light filter through to the forest floor. Strangler figs overcome this problem by clawing their way skyward, while in open glades,

palms compete for the available light.

Unlike the Amazon rainforest, which has more or less constant rainfall throughout the year, Thailand's forests are subject to seasonal bursts of rain from the monsoons. Depending on the geographical position of the forest, some have less than the 80 inches (130cm) of rain a year needed for classic rainforest to develop. In areas with around 50in (80cm) of rain per year, teak can be common, and because of its commercial value it has been the cause of widespread deforestation. Areas on poorly-draining soil may become inundated swamp forest, and to add still further to the variety of habitats, hill forests are different again from lowland rainforest. As the name implies, hill forests normally grow at higher elevations. Because they are often on a slope, the canopy is less dense and the forest floor

Lush forest in the popular Khao Yai National Park, north of Bangkok

Hidden Life

Even a short walk through one of the forests reveals an amazing variety in shape and form of the insects. These adaptations are seldom without a purpose. Often the insect is trying to avoid detection by predators, but occasionally the markings make them more conspicuous, either to warn that the creature is distasteful or to attract a mate. Camouflage is achieved in a variety of ways, some of which are so good that it can be a long time before you notice anything other than the vegetation.

Leaves, bark, twigs and flowers are all mimicked, and some insects even go to the lengths of mimicking discolourations in the vegetation. Most use camouflage to avoid detection by predators but mantids use it to catch their prey. Some look like leaves, while others mimic parts of a flower and lie in wait for visiting insects.

lighter, allowing ferns and orchids to proliferate.

Rainforests support an amazing diversity of plants and animals. In primary Thailand rainforest there might be up to 50 different species of tree in a single acre. The tree canopy in turn helps to maintain a constant high humidity which encourages animals, such as frogs, which would otherwise have to cope with desiccation. Not surprisingly, many of its animals are totally unsuited to life outside the rainforest.

Forest Insects

Thailand's forests are an entomologist's dream come true. There can be few places, with the possible exception of the South American rainforest, that can rival Southeast Asia for the variety and numbers of insects that its forests hold. Literally thousands of different species of insect have already been identified and in all probability hundreds, if not thousands, still remain undescribed.

The diversity of insect life in the forests is due in part to the ideal environmental conditions that prevail and the fact that the climate and food supplies remain good throughout the year. Most of Thailand's insect fauna is typically Southeast Asian in origin, but species from Africa and Australia have also boosted the numbers.

Insects have evolved to exploit every possible source of food in the forest. Different species feed on the leaves, bark, sap, buds, pollen or roots of the trees, while on the forest floor others feed on detritus, dung and even dead animals.

Butterflies and moths are conspicuous and abundant in the forests. Birdwings, swallowtails and atlas moths are among the largest of all flying insects and could easily be mistaken for birds when flying. The adult insects may be showy but by contrast their caterpillars are often camouflaged, blending in perfectly with the leaves on which they feed.

Forest Mammals

Of all Thailand's forest animals, the mammals are perhaps the most difficult to see. Some creatures, such as the slow loris, are largely nocturnal, remaining hidden during the daylight hours, while others, including gibbons, keep high up in the tree canopy. Many of the forest mammals are large and ground-dwelling, and yet are still seldom seen. Tigers, sambar deer and tapirs all keep to the deep shade and their subtle markings increase the effect of camouflage.

The huge, attractive atlas moth can often be seen in the rainforest

Although widely domesticated and used as beasts of burden, Indian elephants were originally forest animals. They can still be seen in some of the national parks, such as Khao Yai, but ironically, in the northern hill regions, they are used to help clear the forests in which they once roamed wild.

Indian elephants are easier to train and better tempered than their African relatives and are almost always the species used in films supposedly set in Africa. The size of the ears gives away their identity: Indian elephants have proportionately much smaller ears.

Gibbons are completely at home in the high canopies of the rainforest. So specialised is their way of life that they cannot survive successfully away from this habitat and are thus seriously threatened by forest clearance. Both lar and pileated gibbons are found in Thailand, feeding on fruits and insects. Gibbons are famous for their agility in the tree tops as they swing gracefully from branch to branch using their powerful arms.

The slow loris is one of Thailand's most unusual and charming animals. Although seldom seen by day, these extraordinary creatures, which look as though they were invented by a cuddly toy designer, can sometimes be observed by torchlight at night. Their large forward-facing eyes, which give them excellent binocular vision, 'glow' when caught in a light. Slow lorises certainly live up to their name, climbing sedately through the trees using enlarged fingerpads

to grip the branches, and hunting slow-moving insects with their well developed sense of smell.

Peninsular Thailand

Stretching 620 miles (1,000km) south from Bangkok to the Malaysian border, peninsular Thailand offers a surprising contrast to the rest of the country. The peninsula possesses a wonderful tropical coastline with aquamarine seas, white sands and palm trees. Tropical forests and densely forested offshore islands add to the variety: a touring holiday down the peninsula can be a marvellous experience.

The drive south from Bangkok is a long one, but fortunately there is plenty to see on the way. Saltpans and marshes, such as those at Lhao Sam Roi Yord, 124 miles (200km) south of the capital and east of Pranburi, hold a superb variety of wading birds, and on the beach there is even a chance of a rarity like great knot or Nordmann's greenshank. Spring bird migration through the peninsula is pronounced and large flocks of oriental pratincoles gather over the saltpans in March and April. Many of the more remote sandy beaches of peninsular Thailand are used as nesting sites by turtles. These immense marine reptiles come ashore at night and lay their eggs in pits dug in the sand. Unfortunately, tourism and turtles do not always mix successfully and many former sites have been deserted. However, Thailand is fortunate in having several protected areas on the peninsula, such as Ang Thong and Tarutao Marine

PEACE AND QUIET

National Parks, and here turtles can nest without disturbance. Nearly 560 miles (900km) south of Bangkok lies Thailand's largest island, Phuket, which from the naturalist's point of view is most rewarding for its seabirds. Boats can be hired for offshore trips, where you can see both greater and lesser frigatebirds and a variety of terns including bridled and crested. Flying fish are a similar sight and dolphins sometimes bow-ride alongside. Turtles are often seen on boat trips, but it is more exciting to see one while snorkelling. The peninsular forest gets better the further south you go. In the superb woods around Krabi you stand a good chance of seeing bat hawks, as well as hornbills, trogons, babblers and woodpeckers. Diminutive mouse deer, intermediates in evolutionary terms between pigs and deer, are shy forest residents which search the forest floor for fallen fruit and are best seen at dawn and dusk.

Khao Yai National Park

Khao Yai is Thailand's best-known and most popular national park. It covers 540,000 acres (218,533ha) of very mixed habitats, with wetlands at around 2,600 feet (800m) above sea level rising to pristine forested hills at 4,387 feet (1,350m). Streams and rivers flow through the park and enchanting waterfalls cascade down hillsides, adding scenic beauty to the charm of its wildlife. Lying only 124 miles (200km) northeast of the capital, Khao Yai is understandably a popular weekend destination for Bangkok

Visitor facilities are good throughout the 540,000 acres of Khao Yai

residents. For the serious wildlife enthusiast a weekday visit might be best, because the more crowded the park is, the further you may have to walk to see the more retiring forest residents. However, whenever you visit the park, and whether you are interested in the wildlife or just the scenery, you are sure not to be disappointed.

Although a single day's visit can be exciting, by staying for a few nights in the park's chalets you can begin to do justice to the magnificent surroundings.

The forests of Khao Yai contain a wealth of interesting plants, with epiphytic orchids and lichens festooning the trees, particularly in the vicinity of water. Exotic ferns and palms add to the feeling that you are in a tropical

jungle and colourful butterflies fly along the glades and rides. Sometimes you may see a group of butterflies apparently drinking from pools on the ground. Nectar contains little apart from sugars, and they are probably more interested in the salts and minerals contained in the water than in the moisture itself. Because of Khao Yai's popularity, the forest around the information centre is disturbed, and yet many of the animals have become accustomed to man's presence. Great-eared nightjars are common around the restaurant at dusk, hawking insects attracted to the lights, while after dark, brown hawk owls frequent the chalets. If you are up for a dawn walk, you may even see a sambar deer on tracks close to the centre. Birdwatching in dense tropical forests can be a bit of a

disappointment at first. Despite all the sounds and calls, it is seemingly impossible even to see the callers, let alone identify them. However, with patience and perseverance, the rewards of Khao Yai's forests will be worthwhile. Silver pheasants and red jungle fowl, the latter an ancestor of the domesticated chicken, still haunt the trails. The first secret to master is that of silence. You will always see much more if you are alone or with a small group of like-minded people. Quietly walk around the trails and listen for calls and rustling leaves. Ground-feeding birds, such as pittas, blue-riband birds for birdwatchers in Asia, make a surprising amount of noise as they turn over leaves in search of food. If you hear a suspicious sound, stand still and wait until the bird comes to you.

Snakes

Hill forest is a rich hunting ground for snakes. Do not be alarmed, however, because in almost all cases snakes prefer to retreat when they hear you. However, Khao Yai's largest snake, the reticulated python, relies upon its camouflage and remains coiled amongst fallen leaves where it is difficult to spot, but towards dusk they sometimes bask on the warm tarmac of the roads in the park. The reticulated python is not only Khao Yai's largest snake, as documented Thai individuals reaching 24 feet (7.5m) rival South America's anaconda for the title of largest snake in the world.

PEACE AND QUIET

The silent approach can also help you to see some of the forest mammals. Elephants still live in Khao Yai and are amazingly quiet for their size, but the ultimate prize for the wildlife enthusiast will undoubtedly be a glimpse of a tiger. Although wary and secretive and seldom seen, they do like to cool off in the heat of the day, and you might see one of these great beasts bathing in a quiet forest stream.

Many of the smaller birds of the tropical forests gather together in mixed flocks outside the breeding season, and these roam through the woods in search of food. With this in mind, the birdwatcher might just as well find a pleasant, open spot and wait for a flock to pass over. One minute there will be nothing to see and the next the binoculars will be scanning wildly through the foliage, desperately trying to identify all the members of the flock.

Northern Thailand

Northern Thailand is a region of hills and mountains and is best explored using Chiang Mai as a base. Lying 435 miles (700km) north of Bangkok, it is within easy reach of several important national parks and high mountains. Although the region has been subjected to considerable forest clearance, there are still many exciting areas.

As well as containing the country's more widespread animals, northern Thailand is strongly influenced by the fauna, and particularly the birds, of the Himalayas. In addition, it provides wintering grounds for thousands of palearctic migrant birds which are far less common in the south of the country.

Doi Inthanon National Park contains Thailand's highest

Tiger – only if you're very lucky will you see one of these

mountain, with a summit at 8,336 feet (2,565m) above sea level, and arguably the most beautiful and dramatic scenery in the whole of the country. From the park entrance, 37 miles (60km) south of Chiang Mai, a road winds its way to the summit. Above an elevation of about 5,850 feet (1,800m), you will begin to notice the epiphytic orchids and lichens which clothe the branches and trunks of the trees, and beautiful waterfalls cascading down narrow valleys. Because of the altitude, temperatures at the summit can be surprisingly chilly, particularly early in the morning, so come prepared. From the car park near the summit, marshes and ravines give way to the forests below and support considerable numbers of winter visitors from northern Asia. From September to March eye-browed thrushes, Siberian rubythroats and a variety of leaf warblers feed alongside resident species. As you descend the mountain stop to explore clearings and ravines, where you may find little green bee-eaters, woodpeckers and wren babblers.

Doi Suthep is the site of a well known temple overlooking Chiang Mai, beyond which are the boundaries of another national park. From the park headquarters, trails lead through the forest to waterfalls and streams. Exotic sounding species like Tickell's babbler, minivets and broadbills add interest to the beautiful terrain. Further up the road beyond Doi Suthep lies Doi Pui, another forested mountain, where visitors may see White's thrush or a daurian redstart on the trails from the viewpoint and picnic site.

The Coast
The Gulf of Thailand is an exotic place for the holidaymaker, especially if he or she is interested in natural history. Sandy beaches lined with palm trees are a constant reminder that you are in the tropics, and mangroves, mudflats and coastal saltpans add to the variety of wildlife habitats.

The mudflats are particularly exciting places, where tens of thousands of migrant waders spend the winter or pass through on migration. Sandplovers, terek and broad-billed sandpipers and kingfishers feed along the shoreline, often in the company of egrets and herons.

Birds are abundant along Thailand's coast because the marine life of the mudflats is rich and plenty of food is available. Mudskippers, curious land-loving fish, are hard to miss as they hop across the mud using their pectoral fins like walking sticks. Their bulging eyes give them good vision and they soon scuttle into the water if danger threatens. Crabs are also abundant. They come in all shapes and sizes, but the most conspicuous and comical are the fiddler crabs, which brandish their brightly-coloured pincers at rivals.

The characteristic tree of the coastal mudflats is the mangrove, and several different species occur in the area. All have evolved to cope with the problems of permanent immersion in seawater and roots

PEACE AND QUIET

buried in thick, anaerobic mud. Apart from Bangpoo – 15 miles (24km) east of Bangkok – other coastal sites worth visiting include the Ko Chang National Marine Park in the east of Thailand. Trat is a centre from which to visit the Chang Islands National Marine Park.

The Lowland Plains
Rice paddies are a familiar feature of lowland Thailand. As a cultivated plant it thrives in the region because this tropical grass probably had its origins in the swamps of Southeast Asia. Young rice plants have to be transplanted to flooded fields, and for ideal growing conditions have to stand in water which is about 6 inches (15cm) deep. From the air, the resulting landscape is a mosaic of watery fields and embankments, providing ideal conditions not only for the crop but also for waterbirds such as cattle and great egrets and open-billed storks, which catch snails, frogs and fish.
In addition to the cultivated wetlands, there are many relatively undisturbed areas within easy reach of Bangkok. At Rangsit, 6 miles (10km) north of Bangkok International Airport, there are marshes with crakes and egrets, while at Wa Tan En, about 56 miles (90km) north of the capital, there is a large colony of open-billed storks. Wherever there are bushes or trees in close proximity to the marshes, you should find heronries and colonies of open-billed storks. These are interesting at any time of the day but in order to see them at their most impressive it is essential to

be there at dawn or dusk, which is unfortunately just the time when the mosquitoes are most active. At dusk you will be treated to the spectacle of vast numbers of fruit bats and night herons leaving for a night's foraging, while diurnal herons and egrets return to roost. At dawn the birds change shift, with the nocturnal birds coming back.

Thailand's Wildlife Hotspots
Bangpoo Marshes (east of Bangkok) – mudflats and mangroves attract migrant and resident shore birds.
Lumphini Park and Chatuchak Park (in Bangkok) – ornamental gardens with common Thai birds.
Ang Thong and Tarutao Marine National Parks (Peninsular Thailand) – beautiful coastline and nesting turtles.
Phuket Island (Peninsular Thailand) – stunning coastline scenery and lots of seabirds and marine life.
Krabi (Peninsular Thailand) – excellent lowland forest.
Khao Yai National Park – excellent hill forest; abundant wildlife includes sambar deer and red jungle fowl.
Doi Inthanon National Park (Northern Thailand) – stunning mountain scenery and forest wildlife.
Doi Suthep (Northern Thailand) – forested mountain trails. Migrant birds from northern Asia winter here.
Rangsit Marshes (north of Bangkok International Airport) – a good area for waterbirds.

Orchids

Orchids belong to one of the most numerous plant families in the world, 27,000 species having been described, over 1,000 of which are found in Thailand: they are a familiar sight in forests, and are also popular in cultivation, as any walk around Bangkok will demonstrate.

Many species grow not in the ground, but on the trunks and branches of trees. These epiphytes, as they are known, have a fleshy root system which grips the tree bark and takes up water and minerals from the surroundings. Tropical orchid flowers produce as many as four million seeds. These lack a food store and rely on a fungal-association in order to germinate, a relationship which most continue throughout their lives. Orchid flowers always comprise three sepals and three petals. The lower lip of the flower is often disproportionately large, making the flower extremely attractive. Although requiring skill and experience, orchid cultivation is straightforward. Regrettably, many plants are simply collected from the wild and sold, resulting in the widespread depletion of attractive species – so don't buy orchid plants unless you are sure they are cultivated.

Vanda Caerulea, *a native of Thailand*

HOW TO BE A LOCAL

Thais are naturally friendly people, but there are a few basic rules:
● Do not point your feet directly at a Thai – it is deeply offensive.
● Always dress discreetly and remove your shoes in a *wat*.
● Thais greet each other with a palms together gesture; if you do likewise you will give considerable pleasure.
● Residents of Bangkok dress formally at night, and in some hotels and restaurants a jacket and tie are necessary.
● Topless bathing is perfectly acceptable, but nude bathing is definitely not.
● Thais are curious people, so will ask you questions that westerners would not normally ask – about your salary, for example. Do not be offended.
● Lastly, enjoy yourself, that's a very Thai thing to do!

WEATHER AND CLOTHES

Cotton clothes, easily washed and dried, are best for Thailand's hot climate. A warm jacket is necessary if visiting the north from November to February. Hat and sunglasses are essential. See also pages 11 and 12.

CHILDREN

The main Thai beach resorts are well equipped for family holidays. Pattaya, in particular, is recommended. Phuket has several children's attractions, such as a large aquarium at the Marine Biological Research Centre. Siam Water Park (10.5 miles or 17km from Bangkok) is a fun-land with roller coaster, water slides and a huge swimming-pool with waves. Magic-Land, the Rose Garden Resort, Dusit Zoo and the Ancient City are all suitable for children.

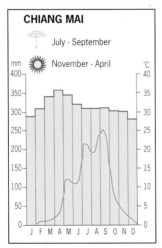

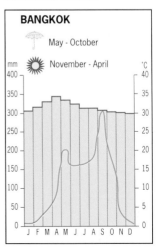

FOOD AND DRINK

(See page 125 for translations of Thai food)

Thai food has become 'trendy' in the west. London has some 40 Thai restaurants, Los Angeles more than 200. Few serve anything like the food in Thailand. Local standards of cooking will only change when more people visit Thailand and demand an improvement on returning home.

Thailand is a place for memorable meals, whether simple food in a fishing village, or an elaborate buffet in a deluxe hotel. It might be accompanied by the sound of waves crashing onto the beach, or *khon* dancers performing on a stage. But it is always good.

Almost all Thai food is cooked with fresh ingredients, with plenty of rice, lemon grass, lime juice and coriander leaves to give its characteristic tang

Thai Cooking

Siam was never conquered, so the fact that Thai cooking resembles an amalgam of several cuisines – most notably Indian, Chinese and Indonesian – is a result of ancient trade links. Foreign dishes became absorbed, to produce a uniquely Thai repertoire which, at the same time, retains the essentials of ethnic, or native food.

Thai food is best described as an Asian version of *nouvelle cuisine*. This is especially true of the Court Cuisine, a refined art once practised exclusively by ladies of the royal household. Tiny portions, exquisitely presented, are usual. But unlike a French chef who drowns a dish in a sauce, a Thai chef serves a dip, in a side bowl. As in *nouvelle cuisine*, appearance is considered as important as taste. Soups arrive with a

FOOD AND DRINK

carved cucumber flower floating on the surface; lotus-shaped carrot buds decorate a bowl of rice. Fruit and vegetable carving is an art: Thai chefs sculpt melons as others carve wood. A Thai buffet table is a tableau to behold.

Thai cooking is, in a word, aromatic: spicy, salty, sour, sweet and at times very hot. Several ingredients are behind its distinctive taste.

The first are chillies; more than a dozen different types are used. The hottest, also the smallest, is a yellow-orange chilli called *phrik khi luang*. Chillies in fish sauce – or *nam pla prik* – is the most common dip. And *nam pla* is to local food what soya sauce is to Chinese meals. A salty, pungent-tasting amber fluid, it is the liquid from fermented fish, mainly anchovies. There is also *nam pla* made from fermented oysters. It sounds terrible, but is delicious. To achieve harmony in a dish, the sharp taste of chilli and spices such as tamarind is often toned down with coconut milk. Not the liquid in a green coconut, but a milk obtained from grating and pressing the white flesh. Coconut milk is used to flavour everything from curries to desserts. Lemon grass is another very popular flavour you will encounter. A famous dish using lemon grass is *tom yum kung,* or seafood soup. Chopped coriander leaves are used as a garnish. A proper Thai meal consists of rice, soup, steamed, fried, stir-fried or grilled fish or poultry (less commonly, meat), a herbed or spiced salad, a vegetable dish and dips, followed by a dessert, but more popularly fresh fruits. This may seem a lot, but people don't usually eat the full menu.

While rice is common to every meal, there are subtle regional variations. In the south, you will find the food is hotter. Based on seafood, it has similarities with Malay food. Northerners prefer milder, less elaborate dishes. They also eat more gelatinous or 'sticky rice', as opposed to steamed rice. *Larp* is widely eaten in northeastern Thailand: made from ground liver, pork or duck with spices and vegetables. Typical vegetables are wing beans, cabbage and aubergines.

Breakfast shows the Chinese influence in Thai cooking. In Bangkok, you should try a typical Thai breakfast at somewhere like the stalls along Sarasin Road, or outside the Central Market. It is usually *khowtom,* or rice with shredded chicken, pork, shrimp and fried garlic served with an egg and pickled cucumbers or other vegetables.

Lunch is usually light. A one-dish affair of fried rice, curry and rice, or mixed noodles and vegetables. Dinner is as described: soup and as many as five other dishes.

Eating in Thailand has no rigid rules. Dishes are served together. Soup can be eaten before, during or after a meal. You can take a mouthful of this or that in any order.

In former times, Thais ate with their hands. People of significant aristocratic

Thai tropical fruits, some of which are less recognisable than others

background would extend their little finger to display the family ring. The spoon and fork used today is said to have been introduced by Rama V (a possible influence of Anna, his children's tutor).

Tables are set with as much care as the cooking and decoration of dishes. Elaborate floral arrangements feature roses and sweetly-scented trumpet flowers. Crockery is often blue and white, or *bencharong,* meaning 'five colours' – another Chinese influence.

Large hotels have menus in English. At street stalls, simply point to what you want.

Thai Fruits

Thailand is renowned for exquisite fruit. You will recognise papaws and mangoes. Others

are less familiar.

● **Durian**: best known for its smell. Some say stench. It is banned in hotels and on planes. The soft, creamy yellow flesh tastes like banana custard and smells like rotten cheese. The huge spiky greenish-yellow fruits ripen from May to August.

- **Mangosteens**: the fruit of the Gods. About the size of a billiard ball, they have smooth, purple skin which stains your hands. Inside are luscious, slightly tart white lobes. The taste is a mix of lychee, mango and passion-fruit. Season May to September.
- **Rambutans**: round, hairy greenish-red fruit. Easily peeled, the flesh is sweet and translucent. Season May to September.
- **Longans**: look boring, but they too are delicious. White flesh similar to a lychee. Season June to August.
- **Jackfruit**: large, pimple-skinned, green and yellow fruit. They grow straight out of the tree trunk on short stalks. Taste between a durian and a custard apple. Season January to May.
- **Custard Apple**: very sweet and pleasant, especially when eaten with ice-cream. Small, pale-green, lumpy-skinned fruit. Season June to September.

Tiny portions, exquisitely served, are typical of Thai Court Cuisine

Thailand grows some of the world's best mangoes. A favourite dessert is sliced mangoes and coconut milk with 'sticky rice'. The fruit of the freshwater lotus is also popular. The Spice Market in the Regent Bangkok Hotel serves coconut custard, caramelised in the shell.

Beverages

Traditional Thai drinks are based on fresh fruit juices made by hawkers cranking ancient presses. Fruit-juice stands are found wherever large numbers of people congregate – at bus-stops, railway stations, outside department stores and the entrances to zoos and parks. Popular juices are mango, sugar-cane and green coconut. No matter how hot, avoid the ice. And do not drink too much juice when you are very hot – it causes cramps and diarrhoea. Never drink tap water.
Local mineral water is good. You will also find familiar soft drinks. Coffee-bars are a growing trend in Bangkok, Pattaya and Phuket. Imported alcohol is very expensive. Local beer is good: *Singha* is like lager, *Kloster* is a soft sweet beer. Local whisky is vile: popular brands are Mekhong and Kwangthong. Thai rum is reasonable. Herbal beverages have a loyal following. Many formulas come from Chiang Mai. You can sample Tiger Power (a potion against insomnia) and Rhinoceros Blood (for special activities and longevity) in the Spice Market in the Regent Bangkok Hotel.

Jim Thompson's shop on Surawongse Road is the place to go in Bangkok for Thai silk

SHOPPING

(See also pages 52-5)

Thailand is one of the best places for shopping in Asia. Not for duty-free goods such as cameras and electrical appliances, but for exquisite local handicrafts. Prices are suited for everyone from a backpacker to a big-spender. Except in fixed-price stores, it is normal to bargain. Try to obtain 15–20 per cent off. Credit cards are widely accepted. If shipping goods, keep your receipts. In case of complaint, contact TAT. Better still, buy in places recommended by TAT, which should display a sign (a girl between two rice baskets on a blue background) – a complete list is available from any TAT office. Avoid street pedlars selling poor-quality goods. Bangkok International Airport has a limited amount of duty-free shopping. The leatherware is good. Prices are usually more expensive than shops. Profiting from the large numbers of tourists, shops at Phuket Airport often charge up to 30 per cent more than local shops, especially for pearls. Never buy anything of value in a hurry.

Thai Silk

Silk-weaving is an old Thai tradition and popular buys are fabric, ties, jackets, shirts, dressing-gowns, napkins and

SHOPPING

cushion covers. You can buy almost anything in Thai silk – jewellery boxes, notebook covers, monogrammed handkerchiefs. A recommended shop is Jim Thompson's at 9 Surawongse Road, which is air-conditioned, with helpful assistants and a great range of merchandise. Seek advice from a local for anything tailor-made, as 24-hour tailors are not always good.

Thai Jewellery

Jewellery-making is an old and respected profession, especially in Bangkok. Burmese rubies and Thai sapphires offer the best value. The star sapphire of Thailand may be blue, grey or black. Other gems are jasper, coral, malachite and turquoise. Beware of fakes: a huge gemstone racket thrives on tourists.

Jewellery comes in a great assortment of necklaces, chains, brooches, earrings and especially rings. Prices range from a few pounds, to thousands. Obtain a certificate of authenticity.

Handicrafts

Popular buys are hand-rubbed teak-ware artefacts, rattan work, macramé, mobiles, brassware and beautifully costumed dolls. Papier-maché *khon* masks are colourful. Silk and rice-paper temple rubbings are light to pack. Have them framed in teak before you leave. Unfortunately many beautiful china objects – vases, lamp-bases and local celadon – are too heavy to take by air. Shipping takes eight to ten weeks, or longer.

Beautiful hand-sculpted and painted papier-maché masks, often copied from temple figures, are true works of art.

Antiques

You are unlikely to buy a bargain-priced antique. The days of a unique find in the Thieves' Market are past. Most dealers know the value, and genuine antiques are museum-priced. Since few people have this budget, the best advice is to buy fakes. Some of the most outstanding examples of Thai craftsmanship are what are known as 'instant antiques'. Perfectly acceptable, they come in wood, bronze, stone and fabric – Burmese, Chinese, Siamese – whatever you fancy. In shops selling both genuine antiques and fakes, simply state you want to buy a copy only. An attractive Buddha image sells

from 600–700 baht. Real works of art require an export permit from the Department of Fine Arts. Ensure the dealer gives you a certificate of guarantee. Except in a reputable shop, you'll probably buy a fake anyway. Two floors of River City in Bangkok specialise in art and antiques with an auction every first Saturday of the month while 'King Antiques', near the Meridien President Hotel, has an excellent range of Thai and Burmese artefacts. Many statues from Burma are effectively stolen temple items smuggled over the border: whether you buy is up to your conscience.

Fakes
This applies equally to fake brand-name watches selling all over Southeast Asia. Thai fakes are considered inferior to Singapore copies. A Gucci may

last a day, a Cartier little longer. Designer copies in leatherware – briefcases, handbags and wallets – are unlikely to stand much use. This goes for the designer-copied clothes you are likely to come across – Lacoste shorts or Calvin Klein jeans.

Clothing
Pratunam Market in Bangkok (opposite the Indra Regent Hotel) is recommended for clothes. Backpackers will find Chiang Mai good for trendy gear such as light cotton trousers and farmers' blue denim shirts, which cost from 40 baht; bargains are found in the Night Bazaar when traders are packing up to go (see page 53).

Hours
Large shops and department stores open daily

10.00–20.00hrs, small shops between 08.00 and 21.00hrs.

Bangkok Shopping Areas

Most tourists shop in the immediate vicinity of their hotel. Unlike most places, hotel shopping arcades are not always more expensive than outside. Bangkok's biggest hotel arcade, almost a mini-city, is within the Indra Regent. Guests staying in the Ploenchit area have the Amarin Plaza, Central Department Store, the Metro Department Store and Narayana Phand Handicrafts (1st floor) shopping mall opposite the World Trade Centre site. Gaysorn Road is one of Bangkok's oldest shopping streets for tourists. Siam Square and Siam Center is a busy area with many boutiques selling clothes, jewellery and handicrafts. Mahaesak-Silom and New Road is another good area to shop. Guests at the riverside hotels – the Oriental, Shangri-La or Royal Orchid Sheraton – can browse in air-conditioned comfort in the River City shopping complex on the Chao Phraya. The plush Oriental Plaza (New Road, behind the Oriental Hotel) offers exclusive shopping.

Markets: Although hot and crowded, Bangkok's markets offer great bargains. Prices are often 50 per cent below even the cheapest shops. Chatuchak (Weekend Market) on Phahon Yothin Road, Bangkok North, is recommended. It sells everything from ducklings to peacock fans, earthenware, army disposal items and bonsai. There are more than 1,000 stalls open every Saturday and Sunday; very crowded after 10.00hrs. Take buses 3, 9, 10 or 13 and alight at the Northern Bus Terminal.

Bang Lam Phu Market sells clothes and other apparel. It is near Kao San Road. Yaowaraj Road is the best place for gold. Bamrung Muang Road (near the Giant Swing) sells religious reliquaries, from giant bronze Buddha images to small items for the home. Behind Wat Rajanada is an amulet market which also sells old coins, statues and other real and fake artefacts.

TIGHT BUDGET

● Newspapers provide a good source of finding cheap charter flights. However, it is very important to ensure the travel agency is a member of IATA and has an ATOL registration number.

● Arriving at Bangkok International Airport, it is wiser to find a bus rather than hire a taxi, since taxi drivers tend to desperately overcharge the naive tourist.

● Budget accommodation is far cheaper if organised on the spot. However, during the peak season be prepared to accept less desirable hotels – especially in the cities.

● Rather than taking an organised tour, find out what it comprises and arrange it independently. For example, hill-tribe treks can be arranged through a budget hotel to relatively undiscovered areas.

● Other travellers can often give useful tips for inexpensive hotels; Banglampoo in Bangkok has cheap accommodation.

Classic Thai dancing, as performed at the Sala Rim Naam restaurant

● For inexpensive shopping, avoid the many tourist traps; learn Thai, and barter.

● Night markets (for example Pratunam in Bangkok, at the junction of Phetchaburi and Rajapraop streets) and street stalls have delicious food, but make sure the cooking area is clean.

● Eat where you see the Thais eating, although this may mean mastering the spices to add to your food.

● Local alcohol, such as Mekong whiskey, is cheaper but stronger than the imported alcohol.

● There are often free performances of traditional Thai dancing in the larger hotels in Bangkok.

● The city buses are sometimes air-conditioned, sometimes not; they vary substantially in price and heat.

● *Tuk-tuks* are a cheaper option than taxis, although bartering is still essential.

EVENTS AND FESTIVALS

Many aspects of Thai culture hold special interest for tourists. The colourful local festivals are a bonus: check what is on when you arrive.

◆◆◆
THAI DANCE-DRAMA

You are bound to see snippets of this here and there, even if you don't attend a performance at the theatre. *Khon,* or masked drama, draws on ancient folk-tales. Common themes come from the epic *Ramakien*, the Thai version of the Hindu *Ramayana*. It would take one month to perform continuously the entire *Ramakien*, with its 311 characters. Shorter, three-hour versions are common. You can see *khon* performances at the dinner show staged nightly from 19.30hrs at the Sala Rim Naam restaurant in Bangkok. Dancers are actors and actresses from the National Theatre and the performance is highly recommended.

Khon has no sets to distract your eye. Each movement is highly exaggerated and each has a different meaning. Actions are precisely timed to music played by a woodwind, drum and gong ensemble. Verses are narrated, as the actors themselves are masked. Lacquered *khon* papier-maché masks are works of art. So too are the heavy brocade costumes duplicating to the finest detail the elaborate, bejewelled regalia worn by temple figures. You can identify the principal characters by their colours: Phra Ram wears a dark green costume, Hanuman the monkey-god is dressed in white. *Lakhon* dance-drama is less formal. The actors do not wear masks and their movements are more fluid. It draws inspiration from the *Ramakien* as well as from ancient Buddhist tales, or *Jatakas*. *Lakhon nai* was originally only performed before ladies of the royal court. A more popular form is a Thai version of the English pantomime. Garishly costumed, often androgynous characters rely on puns and *double entendres*, to loud musical accompaniment. You can see *lakhon* in action at the Lak Muang shrine in Bangkok; performances are free.

The Kodak Show – an event of special interest to photographers – features Thai dancing: Tuesday and Thursday by the pool at the Oriental Hotel at 11.00hrs. In southern Thailand you may chance upon a once-popular *nang talung* shadow play. Sadly the marionettes which entertained ancient Ayutthaya society are today rare. The puppets, however, are sold in handicraft shops.

Muay-Thai *is one of the deadliest forms of unarmed self-defence*

◆◆◆
MUAY-THAI: THAI BOXING

Traditional martial arts survive in the form of sword-fighting and boxing. *Muay-Thai*, or unarmed self-defence, originated in the 1500s when Ayutthaya was a power in Southeast Asia. For many years it formed part of military training for all Thai conscripts. The roughest sport on earth, it is the art of subtle kicks aimed at the throat, knees or solar plexus. The blows have a telling effect: it is not recommended for squeamish spectators. The Thais say the leaping thrusts are scientific. They certainly require rigorous training and discipline. The object is a KO or a points win, and there are few limits beyond kicking below the belt, biting and head-butting. Talking is also forbidden.

It is not the actual contest alone that interests, but the traditions associated with *muay-Thai*. Wearing either blue or red trunks, the contestants kneel to offer prayers. After thanking their teachers, they perform a slow, trance-like dance to music which gains tempo as the bout begins and it not stilled until there is a win.

The referee uses three major words to control the fights: *chok* (fight), *yut* (stop) and *yaek* (break). As for the boxers, when one cries *sok sok* it means he will use his elbows with punishing results. *Kow kow* is a potentially fatal knee-blow. Instant collapse is not uncommon.

Thai boxing consists of five three-minute rounds with two-minute rest intervals. A ten-minute break occurs between each match to enable the audience to place their bets. It is extremely exciting.

You can see *muay-Thai* in two stadiums in Bangkok: Ratchadamnoen Stadium (opposite TAT) on Monday, Wednesday and Thursday at 18.00hrs and Sunday at 17.00hrs. Fights are held in Lumphini Stadium, Rama IV Road, on Tuesday, Friday and Saturday from 18.20hrs. The Rose Garden Cultural Show (15.00hrs daily), see page 36, includes a quick look at Thai-style boxing.

◆◆◆
THAI BULL-FIGHTING

While a bad-tempered bull is a problem for western farmers, peasants in southern Thailand are pleased if one of their herd turns mean. The tussle between bulls, or buffaloes, is a popular rural sport.

Following the rice-harvest, when farmers have less work, talk centres on the stamina and temperament of local bulls. One thing leading to another, a wager is made and a fight arranged. For months prior to the contest, the animals follow a strict training scheme.

Initially, the bull is allowed to roam to assert his independence. He is then captured and real training begins: light morning jogging along the beach to strengthen his legs, a rub-down and a siesta. Diet is lush grasses and raw eggs – as many as 15 a day. At night he is housed inside an insect-proof pen (it is

Although bull-fights are serious entertainment mock fights are staged at some tourist centres

said that one mosquito in a night's feed can weaken a fighting bull). Dates of the fight are posted around the village and owners confer as to how to pair the bulls.

The arena is usually a makeshift ring in a rural clearing. Spectators crowd the rails and perch in trees. When everyone is ready, trainers lead in their animals garlanded with flowers and smeared with 'magic' paste. Their satin cloaks are removed, helpers scale the barrier, a gong sounds, and the owners swing the bulls round for eye contact.

Pawing the dust, they charge with an audible clonk of horns. Backing away, they charge again. And again. A contest may last for hours. On the other hand, a cowardly bull may suddenly break away. If their horns become locked, the fight is declared a draw. If one bull falls down and does not get up within five minutes, the other is declared the winner. The owner is permitted to beat only his own bull.

Apart from kite-fighting, bull-fighting is the only entertainment for many farmers. In the old days a bottle of rice wine or a basket of eggs was wagered on a contest. Today, thousands of baht are bet. Songkhla is the bull-fight capital of Thailand. Fights are also staged on Ko Samui. On most occasions you will see a fight posted only by chance. The programme at the Rose Garden Resort (see page 36) features mock bull-fights.

SIAMESE FIGHTING FISH

People are equally thrilled by a bout between two pugnacious fighting fish as they are between a pair of bulls. Fish-fighting is a native sport, now banned in Bangkok, but popular in the countryside. Breeders bring their current champions in small jars. The fish are paired according to the measure of animosity displayed through the glass. Bets are placed on the reactions. Put in an aquarium, the chosen pair waste no time in savagely attacking each other. Fins, scales and bits of their lovely flowing tails are ripped off. Sometimes their jaws become locked for minutes, even hours. It is a fight to the death of one fish. There are no draws. You will see Siamese fighting fish on sale in Bangkok's Chatuchak (Weekend Market).

◆ KITE-FIGHTING

The summer winds which herald the kite-fighting season are eagerly awaited. Especially at weekends between February and April, contests are held on the Pramane Ground, opposite

Hundreds of highly-coloured kites waiting to fly and fight

the Grand Palace, in Bangkok. Anyone can own a kite. The cheapest are made of string and paper, but it is the huge, colourful male *chula* and female *pakpao* kites which draw most onlookers. Kites in fact can take hundreds of different forms – birds, fish, faces. In size they range from just one or two inches, or 30 or more feet (a few centimetres, to 9–10 metres), which require several people to lift.

Rules governing kite-fighting contests are rather complex and, like boxing or fish fights, everyone bets on the outcome. A *chula* team comprises the captain, a handler – the kite flyer – and a team of agile boys who obey the captain's whistle. Strips of bamboo hooks along the string are to entangle other kites. The more feminine looking *pakpao* uses a long,

starched tail as a snare together with a loop hanging from the string that flies her. Speed and agility are her main defence in combat with the ponderous *chula* kites. A championship contest draws large crowds, particularly in rural Thailand where entertainment is rare. Sold on Pramane Ground, kites make good souvenirs.

◆◆◆

SURIN ELEPHANT ROUND-UP

Elephants occupy a special niche in Thai history. Rare albino elephants were considered royal, and were ridden only by the king. Erawan – the triple-headed elephant of Thai mythology – is seen everywhere. Tiny carvings are left on spirit houses, huge statues are placed at shrines. Originally trained for war, elephants are still used for lumbering in the north. You can visit Elephant Village 31 miles (50km) from town. Wild elephants used to be hunted along Thailand's border with Cambodia by men of the Suay tribe, 'elephant people', who followed strict rules. About 50 tame animals, each with two riders, took part in a round-up lasting two or three months. Offerings were made to thick buffalo-hide ropes used to capture the herd. The men had to confess misdemeanours to a chief. If guilty, they were thrown in the river, or made to crawl carrying the heavy rope, or *nang pakam*. This acted as an exorcism.

From a base-camp in wild-

elephant territory, daily sorties were made after a herd. When the tame elephant drew close, the first mahout lassooed the wild beast's leg and secured it to a forest giant. The tame elephant took the wild one's weight as it plunged and trumpeted in the undergrowth. After 10 or 12 days without food or water, the wild elephant was ready to be taken to the village, where a tame animal led the dispirited pachyderm into a *kraal* for breaking in. This took from two to six weeks. Accidents on a hunt were blamed on Suay womenfolk. Left at home, they also had rules. They could not cut their hair, or sit on the steps of their house. People still believe such mumbo-jumbo in Ban Ta Klang, Tambon Krapho and other elephant villages in Surin province, 295 miles (475km) northeast of Bangkok. Well trained by mahouts from this area, over 100 elephants take part in the annual round-up organised by TAT in Surin. Although commercial, it is well organised. Held on the third weekend of November, it features elephant races, a tug-o'-war, logging, a simulated hunt and a war-parade. A TAT package includes train fare, first-class sleeper, meals, transfers and admission: depart Bangkok 08.45hrs, arrive Surin 06.00hrs the next day.

Independent travellers are recommended to the Petchkasem, Memorial and Amarin hotels. All are comfortable, but fairly noisy. Advance booking is essential.

Some of the inmates at Samut Prakan Crocodile Farm

◆
SAMUT PRAKAN CROCODILE FARM

The Samut Prakan Crocodile Farm is located 18.5 miles (30km) from Bangkok near the mouth of the Pak Nam river. There are many crocodiles, both fresh- and salt-water species, as well as South American caimans and one or two from the Nile. They range from babies to 13-foot (4m) monsters. All get turned into handbags and shoes. There are shows every hour from 09.00–11.00hrs and 14.00–16.00hrs, with additional shows at 17.00hrs at weekends. The best time to go is at feeding time: 16.30–17.30hrs. Both are good value for children.

The farm has a small zoo where some of Thailand's indigenous creatures are kept in miserable cages. There are refreshments, toilets and a shop selling crocodile skin products. Open 09.00–18.00hrs, admission charge. From the capital, take buses 25, 45, 119 or 102 to Samut Prakan, then take mini-bus number S1-S55. The farm can be visited *en route* to Pattaya.

Festivals

Commemorative and celebrative festivals are an important feature of Thai life. Most are linked with the Buddhist religion and the agricultural cycle, in particular rice-farming. Some occur on fixed dates, others change with the lunar calendar. Most occur in the cool season: November–February.
* Indicates a national holiday.

- **Chiang Mai Flower Festival**: annually, when local flowers are in full bloom, there are floral floats and displays. Held every second Friday, Saturday and Sunday during February.
- ***Makha Bucha**: Buddhist All Saints' Day, this commemorates the occasion when 1,250 disciples gathered spontaneously to hear Buddha preach. At dusk throughout the country, Buddhist monks lead triple circumambulations of *bots*. People carry a candle, incense and flowers in silent homage to Buddha. Birds are also released. A national holiday, *Makha Bucha* falls on the day of the full moon of the third lunar month (late February to early March).
- **The Dove Festival**: held in Yala, this attracts competitors from all the ASEAN countries. In particular, more than 1,400 people enter a dove cooing contest. Bazaars and sports. Held in early March.
- **Phra Buddha Bat**: when Buddhist devotees flock to the Holy Footprint Shrine mount near Saraburi, 85 miles (136km) north of Bangkok. Folk music and bazaars. Early March.
- **Pattaya Festival**: beauty contests, floats, fireworks and

Candles have a special place in commemorative and religious festivals

other attractions. Mid April.
- ***Songkran**: essentially a religious holiday marking the Buddhist New Year. Traditionally Thais visit the temple and clean their house. More recently, it is the occasion for a sudden drenching. Water-throwing and other merriment occurs, especially in Chiang Mai and Samut Prakan. You too may be a target but it is welcome in April (between 13th–15th), the hottest month of the year.
- **Rocket Festival**: villagers in Thailand's northeast province fire giant, homemade rockets to encourage bountiful rains during the rice-growing season. Best seen at Yasothon. Second weekend in May.
- ***Royal Ploughing**

Ceremony: Presided over by HM King Bhumiphol in Bangkok, this marks the official start of the rice-growing season. At Brahman rituals sacred cows are offered rice, grasses and water. Their willingness to eat and drink indicates the harvest ahead. Early to mid May.

● ***Visakha Bucha**: the most sacred of all Buddhist occasions commemorates Buddha's birth, enlightenment and death. Various ceremonies and candlelit processions. Held on the full moon of the sixth lunar month (May or June).

● **Fruit Fair**: colourful displays of local fruits, exhibitions and folklore. Late May to early June. Held in Rayong, Chantha Buri, Chachoengsao, Hat Yai and Songkhla.

● ***Asanaha Bucha**: marks the start of Buddhist Lent, *Khao Phansa* (Rains Retreat), when monks withdraw into the *wats* to meditate for three months during the rains. Novices throw a party on the night before their ordination. Next day they receive the saffron robes of a monk. *Tak Bat Dok Mai,* or merit-making festival, coincides with the rains retreat. Lay people make offerings at the shrines. Occurs at the end of July or early August.

● **Candle Festival**: most grandly celebrated in Ubon Ratchathani in northeastern Thailand. The town of Ubon stages: floats, food stalls, beauty contests and processions of huge carved candles – human, animal and divine. The festival begins around the day after *Asanaha Bucha* (see above) and lasts three days.

● **Phra Pathom Chedi Fair**: annual bazaar featuring foods, fruits and floral parades in Nakhon Pathom. Early September.

● **Kin Kuai Salek**: traditional northern Thai festival where women make offerings of foods and spices in wicker baskets and decorated trays. Each contains a note from the girl to the person to whom the merit is dedicated. Temple processions. September.

● **Lanna Boat-races**: spectacular rowing-races in traditional boats at Nan, 490 miles (790km) north of Bangkok. Regattas in Suratthani and Pathumthani. Mid October.

● **Chak Phra Festival**: a Buddha image is pulled on a carriage through Suratthani. Late October to early November.

● **Thot Kathin**: takes place

after Lent when new robes are brought to the monks by laymen. Usually the king leads the example. In past years he led a barge procession to Wat Arun in Bangkok. In mid-October to mid-November, after Lent.

● **Surin Elephant Round-Up**: colourful programme of folklore and elephant feats at Surin in northeastern Thailand. Third weekend in November (see also page 110).

● **Loy Krathong**: the most famous and beautiful of all Thai festivals. A *krathong* (a small, lotus-shaped boat containing a candle, an incense stick and a coin) is launched on a stream or the sea. The act pays homage to the water spirits and atones for any sins. It is held throughout

A 'war elephant' parade: a tourist treat in Surin, northeast Thailand

Thailand – girls even leave their bars in Pattaya and Phuket to release their *krathongs*. Riverside hotels in Bangkok and Lumphini Park are good vantage points. In Chiang Mai there is a city-wide festival. Held on the night of the full moon in November.

● **Golden Mount Fair**: candlelit procession up Wat Sakhet to the Golden Mount in Bangkok. Food stalls and open-air theatre around the base. November.

● **River Kwai Bridge Week**: *son et lumière* at the bridge over the River Kwai at Kanchana Buri. Exhibitions, food stalls, steam-train rides. Late November to early December.

● ***HM The King's Birthday**: a national holiday on 5 December. Fireworks, decorations and floodlights on Ratchadamnoen Avenue in Bangkok.

DIRECTORY

Arriving

By Air: More than 45 airlines and charter companies fly to Bangkok. (Many also go to Phuket.) The national carrier, Thai Airways International, is highly regarded by frequent travellers. There are regular flights from all western countries. Those wishing to travel at a discount will be able to find cheap flights without difficulty.

Bangkok International Airport, 14 miles (22km) outside Bangkok, has long treks to immigration and a cramped departures hall. But duty-free facilities are good and security is excellent. Chiang Mai has a good new airport. Facilities at Phuket are being upgraded. There are also flights to Hat Yai and U-Taphao for Pattaya. The journey into Bangkok from the airport takes a minimum 45 minutes by car, or up to an hour

Bangkok seems at first to be one big polluted, noisy traffic-jam

and a half by bus. Airport buses depart every 20 minutes; there are also air-conditioned limousines. Taxis are located outside the airport; they are unmetered, and you must agree on a fare which should not exceed 200 baht. Backpackers can catch bus 59 to the National Monument in Rajadamnoen Avenue. It is then a short walk to Khao San Road, a cheap accommodation area.

There is an international departure tax from Thailand.

By Rail: Good, air-conditioned express trains operate between Singapore, Kuala Lumpur (Malaysia) and Bangkok. Second-class sleepers are comfortable but must be reserved in advance. The journey takes a day and a half. Call Bangkok 02 2237010 or 2237020 for information.

By Road: Overland travel to Thailand is only possible via Malaysia. VIP and air-conditioned buses operate between Thailand and Malaysia (notably Kuala Lumpur and Penang) and Singapore.

Entry Formalities: Visitors holding passports of most countries are permitted to stay in Thailand for up to 15 days without a visa.

New Zealand passport holders can stay up to three months without a visa.

Length of Stay: Without visa, with confirmed onward or return ticket, 15 days. With transit visa, 30 days. With tourist visa, 60 days. With non-immigrant visa, 90 days. Extensions of transit and tourist visas can be requested at immigration offices. Overstaying your visa will result in an automatic fine of 100 baht per day, payable on departure. No exit visa is required.

Customs Regulations

You may import 200 cigarettes, or tobacco not exceeding 250 grammes, and 1 litre of spirits or wine. Regulations stipulate one still camera and five rolls of film, but customs are relaxed on this point. You may import any amount of foreign currency, but amounts in excess of US$10,000 must be declared. Up to 50,000 baht per person may be taken out.

Flying is by far the best way of travelling long distances in Thailand

Driving
Car Rental

It is possible to rent cars (or jeeps) in Bangkok, Pattaya, Chaing Mai, Phuket, Hat Yai and Samui Island. An international licence is required and you must be over 21. Driving is on the left. When rules are observed, they generally follow the UK code.

Thailand has nearly 31,000 miles or 50,000km of reasonably good roads and two-lane highways. Highway tolls range from 10 baht. Having said this, self-drive in Thailand is not advised. The Thais are second to the Malays as the worst drivers in Asia. Trucks make long journeys hazardous. Speed limits are 37mph (60kph) in towns, 62mph (100kph) outside towns and 49mph (80kph) on Bangkok expressways, although few drivers take much notice. Phuket and the quiet roads around Chiang Mai are the only areas where self-drive is feasible. Avis and Hertz can also offer chauffeur-driven vehicles.

Avis

Bangkok, 10/1 North Sathorn Road (tel: 02 2330397).
Chiang Mai, 14/14 Huay Kaew Road (tel: 053 222013).
Koh Samui, Imperial Samui Hotel (tel: 077 421390).
Phuket, opposite Phuket Airport (tel: 076 311358).

Hertz

Bangkok, 1620 New Petchaburi Road (tel: 02 2517575).
Chiang Mai, 12/3 Loi Khlao Road (tel: 053 235925).
Phuket, opposite Phuket Airport (tel: 076 311162).

Car owners travelling overland through Thailand must have in their possession:
1) a valid international licence, or equivalent document
2) vehicle registration documents
3) a cash or bank guarantee if the car is brought in through Bangkok Airport or Port Klong Tuey.
If entry is by land across the southern border, completion of regulation customs forms is sufficient. Permission is granted for a six-month stay. Short stays can be extended free of charge by the Customs Department.

Note: the Burmese border is closed to all overland traffic.

Electricity

220 volts/50 cycles, though different-style connections may be encountered throughout the country (bring an adaptor).

Embassies

Australian Embassy, 37 Sathorn Tai Road, Bangkok (tel: 02 2872680).
British Embassy, 1031 Wireless Road, Bangkok (tel: 02 2530191).
Canadian Embassy, 11th & 12th Floors, Boonmitr Building, 138 Silom Road, Bangkok (tel: 02 2374126).
Embassy of the United States of America, 95 Wireless Road, Bangkok (tel: 02 2525040).
Irish Embassy, United Flourmill Building, 11th Floor, 205 Ratchawongse Road, Bangkok (tel: 02 2230876).
New Zealand Embassy, 93 Wireless Road, Bangkok (tel: 02 2518165).

DIRECTORY

Emergency Telephone Numbers
Police: 191
Tourist Police: 195
Fire: 199
Ambulance (Bangkok): 02 2522171-5
Highway Police: 02 2816240-1
Tourist Assistance: 02 2815051

Health Regulations
No vaccinations are required unless you are coming from an infected zone. Malarial prophylactics are essential outside Bangkok.

Lost Property
There is a 24-hour lost property office at Bangkok International Airport, situated in the arrivals lounge (tel: 02 5352173, 5352811-2). Anything left in a taxi can be recovered more quickly if you know the taxi's number – make a note of it.

Money Matters
Currency: the Thai *baht*. Paper notes are in denominations of 500, 100, 50, 20 and 10. Coins are 25 and 50 *satangs* (100 = 1 *baht*) and 1, 2, 5 and 10 *baht*. Small notes are advised as getting change for a 500 *baht* note can be difficult in places. General banking hours are Monday–Friday 08.30–15.30hrs but major banks operate currency exchange centres in most tourist areas, daily (including holidays) from 07.00 to 21.00hrs. Exchange facilities exist at Bangkok International Airport (24 hours). Exchange dealers offer the best rates and stay open until 20.00 or 21.00hrs. Major credit cards are widely negotiable throughout Thailand. Use cash when bargaining.

Opening Times
Government Offices: Monday–Friday, 08.30hrs–noon and 13.00–16.30hrs.
Post Office: (see **Post Office**)
Banks: (see **Money Matters**)
Shops: Large shops and departments stores daily 10.00–20.00hrs, small shops between 08.00 and 21.00hrs
National Museums: Generally Wednesday–Sunday 08.30–12.00hrs and 13.00–16.30hrs (closed Monday, Tuesday and public holidays).

Personal Safety
Thailand is a malarial zone, though some districts are reputedly worse than others. Take precautions before, during and for six weeks following your return. You should also take with you a good mosquito repellent such as 'Repel 100'. Backpackers planning to camp should be extra careful.

The unit of currency in Thailand is the baht: notes are valued at 10, 100, 20, 50 and 500 baht (clockwise, from top right)

Wearing a long-sleeve shirt and trousers after dark lessens the area vulnerable to bites. You may go to Thailand and never see a mosquito.
Creepie-crawlies are encountered on hill treks. Most are not dangerous but beware of sea urchins on the coast. Treading on one will ruin your holiday. Watch that coral cuts do not become infected. And watch the sun. It burns quickly in the tropics. Use high-protection sunscreen. Wear a hat and shirt when out on the water.
Gamble on getting diarrhoea. It is usually your stomach's reaction to chillies or because you've been drinking unbottled water. Abstain from eating for a day: fresh coconut juice may

help. Take anti-diarrhoea tablets (Tannalbine are good). If runs persist, see a doctor. If you burn your mouth on a chilli, ask for rice, not water: chilled fluid makes it worse. Beware of chills. When tired from travelling, the body does not adjust to sudden changes in temperature. Air-conditioned hotels are always too cold. Wear a sweater when you come inside. Never sleep without adequate cover.

Public Holidays
1 January: New Year's Day
Mid to late February: Chinese New Year's Day
Late February to early March: Makha Bucha
6 April: Chakri Day
Mid April: Songkran (Thai New Year)
1 May: National Labour Day
5 May: Coronation Day
Early to mid May: Royal Ploughing Ceremony
May–June: Visakha Bucha
Late July: Asanaha Bucha
Late July: Khao Phansa
12 August: Queen's Birthday
23 October: Chulalongkorn Day
5 December: King's Birthday
10 December: Constitution Day
31 December: New Year's Eve

Public Transport
The internal airline is Thai Airways. An extremely good carrier, it flies to all major towns in Thailand. Food and refreshments are served on all flights. Domestic departure tax is 20 baht. Baggage limit, 20kg tourist class.
Thai trains are clean, comfortable and run on time. Train travel is far less stressful than the congested roads. Good food is available from vendors

all along the line. People wishing to be most comfortable should travel first class. Reservations must be made in advance. Air-conditioned sleepers are available for long journeys. Visitors may purchase a 20-day pass permitting unlimited second and third-class travel throughout Thailand. Timetables are available from Bangkok's Hualumpong Station: for information telephone 02 2237010 or 2237020, reservations 02 2233762 or 2247788.

Air-conditioned buses and ordinary buses operate all over Thailand. You usually need a day to recover from the experience. Major bus terminals are Taladmochit, Paholyothin Road (north and northeastern routes); Ekami, Sukhumvit Road (eastern routes); and Sai tai, Nakhon Chaisri Road (southern routes). You may waste hours getting to these stops. The best idea is to take a *tuk-tuk,* or a taxi. Ask your hotel concierge to write down the name of the stop in Thai as well as telling the driver where you are going. *Tuk-tuks* are hot, noisy, three-wheel motorbike taxis. Driven with a reckless regard for

human life, they are quicker than other motorised transport. The fare in Bangkok should not exceed 150 baht. Forget city buses. Crowded with hapless commuters, they experience terrible delays. Pedi-cabs are a relaxed means of transport in some rural towns.

People with the time and inclination can travel considerable distances by river. Many changes of boat are involved and a working

Thais greet each other, with a prayer-like gesture, palms together, known as a wai

knowledge of Thai is essential. Backpackers will enjoy it, but take a change of clothes as you will not stay dry.

Student and Youth Travel

Unlimited second-class travel on Thailand's railways for 7, 14 or 21 days is possible with the Eurotrain Explorer Pass, available to students and those under 30 years, from major student and youth travel bureaux worldwide.

Time

Thailand is seven hours ahead of Greenwich Mean Time. Thailand observes the western 12-month calendar. Religious and seasonal ceremonies follow lunar time.

Telephone

Local calls can be made from any telephone. Long-distance domestic calls require a blue call box. Phones take 1 and 5 baht coins. International calls can be made from major post offices, private telephone offices and hotels. Dial 001, followed by the country code (Australia 61; Canada and the US 1; Ireland 353; New Zealand 64; Britain 44). For an English-speaking operator dial 13.

Tipping

Tipping is unnecessary in simple places, but in up-market hotels you should give 10–20 baht to porters. In larger restaurants tip 5–10 per cent, in smaller ones a 10 or 20 baht note is adequate. It is usual to tip hairdressers 5–10 per cent and guides 10–20 per cent. Do not tip taxis. US dollar notes are useful to carry since the demise of the sterling pound note.

DIRECTORY

Tourism Authority of Thailand (TAT)
Australia
Sydney Royal Exchange Building, 56 Pitt Street, Sydney 2000 (tel: 02 247 7549).
Britain
London 49 Albemarle Street, London W1X 3FE (tel: 071 499 7679).
US
New York 5 World Trade Centre, Suite 3443, New York, NY 10048 (tel: 212 432 0433).
Los Angeles 3440 Wilshire Boulevard, Suite 1100, Los Angeles, CA 90010 (tel: 213 382 2353).
Chicago 303 East Wacker Drive, Suite 400, Chicago IL 60601 (tel: 312 819 3990).
Thailand
Head Office 372 Bamrung Muang Road, Bangkok 10100 (tel: 02 2260060, 2260072, 2260085, 2260098).
Central
Cha-Am 500/1 Phetkasem Road (tel: 032 471005-6).
Kanchana Buri Saeng Chuto Road (tel: 034 511200).
Pattaya 382/1 Chaihat Road, South Pattaya (tel: 038 428750)
Rayong 300/77 Liang Muang Road (tel: 038 611228).
North
Chiang Mai 105/1 Chiang Mai – Lamphun Road (tel: 053 248604, 248607).
Chiang-Rai 448/16 Singhaclai Road (tel: 053 717433).
Northeast
Nakhon Ratchasima 2102 Mittraphap Road (tel: 044 213666).
South
Hat Yai 1/1 Soi 2 Niphat Uthit 3 Road (tel: 074 243747, 238518, 231055).

Nakhon Si Thammarat 1180 Bowon Bazaar, Ratchadamnoen Road (tel: 075 356356).
Phuket 73-75 Phuket Road (tel: 076 212213, 211036).
Suratthani 5 Talat Mai Road, Ban Don (tel: 077 281828).

Travel Agencies and Tour Companies
Bangkok
Arlymear Travel 6th Floor CCT Bldg, 109 Surawongse Road, Bangkok 10500 (tel: 02 2369317).
Arosa Travel Service 5th Floor Kongboonma Bldg, 699 Silom Road, Bangkok 10500 (tel: 02 2340983, 2334526).
Asian Tours Center 5th Floor British Airways Building, 113/19 Gaysorn Road, Bangkok 10330 (tel: 02 2529388, 2525889).
Boon Vanit 420/9-10 Siam Square Soi 1, Rama I Road, Bangkok 10330 (tel: 02 2510526, 2520151, 2527892).
C & F Travel 3036 Indra Shopping Arcade, Rajprarob, Bangkok 10400 (tel: 02 2531288).
Diethelm Travel Kian Gwan Bldg II, 140/1 Wireless Road, Bangkok 10330 (tel: 02 2559150).
East West Tours 135 Soi Sanam Khli (Soi Polo), Wireless Road, Bangkok 10330 (tel: 02 2530681).
Federal Travel 131/19-20 Sukhumvit Road, Soi 9, Bangkok 10110 (tel: 02 2512155).
Pacific Leisure 518/2 Maneeye Bldg, Ploenchit Road, Bangkok 10330 (tel: 02 2511393, 2523520).
Sea Tours Suite 413-4 (4th Floor) Siam Center, 965 Rama I Road, Bangkok 10330 (tel: 02 2514862).
Siam Express 14th Floor, 90/34-35 Sathornthani Bldg, Sathorn Nua Road, Bangkok 10500 (tel: 02 2365970).
Siam Friendship Tours 5/1 Dejo

Some public buses are slow; others (rot tua or tour buses) are faster; all are cheap

Road, Silom, Bangkok 10500 (tel: 02 2350100).
Thai International Tours 21st Floor, Charn Issara Tower Bldg, 942/163 Rama IV Road, Bangkok 10500 (tel: 02 2354100).
Thaisinn Express Room 1106, Wall Street Tower, 33 Surawongse Road, Bangkok 10500 (tel: 02 2330797, 2367974).
Tour East 4th Floor Hong Kong Bang Bldg, 64 Silom Road, Bangkok 10500 (tel: 02 2354020).
Tour Royal International: 28/2-3 Watana Lane, 19 Sukhumvit, Bangkok 10110 (tel: 02 2530600, 2532886).
Turismo Thai 511 Si Ayutthaya Road, Phayathai, Bangkok 10400 (tel: 02 2451551, 2452937).
Travex 82/5 Soi Lang Suan, Ploenchit Road, Bangkok 10330 (tel: 02 2513504, 2510761).
World Travel Service 1053 Charoen Krung Road, Bangkok 10500 (tel: 02 2335900)
Diethelm Travel, Turismo Thai, Tour Royal International and World Travel Service are especially recommended.

Chiang Mai
Chiang Mai Golden Tours c/o Phornphing Hotel, Charoenprathet Road, (tel: 053 235099).
Discovery Tours Poy Luang Hotel, (tel: 053 234633).
MEI Tour c/o Montri Hotel, Rajdamnoen Road (tel: 053 234358).
North West Tours c/o Suriwongse Hotel, Changkhlan Road (tel: 053 236789, 236733).
Thai International Tours c/o Chiang Inn Hotel, Changkhlan Road (tel: 053 235655).
Tourismo-Thai c/o Chiang Inn Hotel, Changkhlan road (tel: 053 235655).
World Travel Service c/o Rincome Hotel, Huay Kaew Road (tel: 053 221044).

LANGUAGE

Although many young Thais speak English, communications are often difficult. A few words of Thai will help but it is a complex language to learn: there are 44 consonants, 38 vowels and five different tones. Below are a few useful words and phrases.

Numbers

1	Nueng
2	Song
3	Saam
4	See
5	Haa
6	Hok
7	Jet
8	Baat
9	Gao
10	Sip
11	Sip-et
12	Sip-song
13	Sip-saam
14	Sip-see
15	Sip-haa
16	Sip-hok
17	Sip-jet
18	Sip-baat
19	Sip-gao
20	Yee-sip
21	Yee-sip-et
30	Saam-sip
100	Neung roi
1,000	Neung paan
10,000	Neung meun

Basic Phrases

Thank you Kop koon krap (male), Kop koon kaa (female)
Hello, goodbye Sawat-dee (krap, kaa)
It doesn't matter Mai pen rai
Yes Chai (or krap, kaa)
No Mai
How are you? Sabai dee reu?
I'm not feeling well Mai sabai (krap, kaa)

I'm fine Sabai dee (krap, kaa)
I understand Kao chai
I don't understand Mai kao chai
Do you understand? Kao chai mai?
Too expensive Paeng bai
A little Nit noy

Questions

What is your name? Koon cheu arai (krap)?
My name is... Pome cheu... (male) Chan cheu... (female)
How much does this cost? Nee tao-rai (krap, kaa)?
Do you have... mee mai?
What is this? Nee arai?
Where is the washroom? Hong nam yuu nai?

Directions

I want to go ... Yaak ja py...
Where is...? yuu nai?
Turn left Leeo sy
Turn right Leeo kwaa
Straight ahead Trong by
Stop here Yuut tee nee

Time

Today Wan nee
Tomorrow Pruung nee
Yesterday Meua wan nee

Places

Airport Sanaam bin
Bathroom Hong nam
Beach Haat
Bus station Sa-tanee rot mae
Country Prataet
Embassy Sa-tantoot
Hospital Rong payabaan
Hotel Rong raem
Island Koh
Market Talaat
Police station Sa-tanee tumruat
Post office Praisanee
Railway station Sa-tanee rot fai
River Maenam
Town Meuang

General
Water-serpent from Hindu mythology Naga
Mythical bird Garuda
Spire Prang
Pagoda Chedi
Canal, pond Klong
Buddhist monastery Wat
Main chapel of a wat Bot
Secondary chapel of a wat Viharn
Pagoda-type structure Stupa
Open-sided pavilion Sala
Masked drama Khon
Pedal-taxi Samlor
Motorbike taxi Tuk-tuk
Lane Soi
Pick-up van converted to bus or mini-bus Son tao
Foreigner Farang

Food
Beef Neua
Chicken Gai
Chillies Prik
Coffee Gafae
Eggs Kai
Salted eggs Khai kem
Fish Pla
Fish sauce Naam pla
Shrimp paste Kapi
Dried fish Pla haeng
Dried shrimp Ghoong haeng
Salted fish Pla kem
Pork Muu
Rice Khow
Sticky rice Khow niaw
Salt Gluea
Sugar Naam taan
Palm sugar Naam taan peep
Sweet Waan
Tea Chaa
Water Nam
Tamarind Ma kaam
Coconut Ma prow
Noodles Guay tiaw
Vermicelli Sen mee
Jelly or glass noodles Woon sen
Egg noodles Ba mee
Bean curd Tao hoo
Salted soya beans Tao jiaw

Fruits *(ponlamai)*
Durian Thurian
Palmyra Loog taan
Water chestnuts Haew
Banana Gluay
Mango Ma muang
Papaya Mala kaw
Orange Som
Lychee Linchee
Rose apple Chompoo
Crab apple Pood sa
Guava Farang
Mangosteen Mung kood
Custard apple Noi na
Jackfruit Kha noon
Rambutans Ngaw

Vegetables
Beansprouts Thua ngok
Aubergine Ma khuea yow
Mushrooms Hed
Water spinach Park boong
Winter melon Fug
White radishes/turnips Hua pakkaad
Pumpkin Fug thong
Gourd Mara
Ribbed gourd Buab
Cucumber Taeng kwa

INDEX

ACKNOWLEDGEMENTS

ACKNOWLEDGEMENTS

The Automobile Association would like to thank the following photographers and libraries for their assistance in the compilation of this book

INTERNATIONAL PHOTOBANK Cover Bangkok, 10 Rice Barge Cruise, 64 Asia Pattaya Hotel, 79 Le Meridien Hotel.

NATURE PHOTOGRAPHERS LTD S C Bisserot 86 Fruit Bat, 88 Atlas Moth, B Burbidge 95 Vanda Caeruhea, J Hancock, 92 Tiger, C K Mylne 85 Flowering Tree, 87 Forest Path, 90/1 Khao Yai N.P.

CHRISTINE OSBORNE PICTURES 8 Monks, 12 Clothing Industry, 13 Rice Harvest, 15 Lumphini Park, 17 Grand Palace, 18 Wat Phra Kaeo, 20 Temple of the Golden Mount, 23 Vimanmek, 24 Flower Seller, 28 Regent Bangkok Hotel, 30 Oriental Hotel Ent., 32 Food Vendor, 34 Transvestite Show, 36 Rose Garden Resort, 38 Kanchanaburi War Cemetery, 40 Ayutthaya, 42 Rice Planting, 45 Cha-Am, 49 Mural Wat Chiang Mai, 50 Weaving Hill Tribe, 52 Baskets, village of Hang Dong, 54 Parasols Chiang Mai, 57 Elephant, 61 Salt Mining, 63 Bang Saen, 67 Neon Signs, 68 Fish Market, 71 Phuket Market, 72 Koh Samui, 74 Monkey Spinner, Coconut, 80 Shell Fossils Krabi, 82 Phi Phi Lae, 83 Phi Phi Don Beach, 84 Nests Koh Phi Phi, 97 Thai Food, 99 Tropical Fruits, 100 Royal Thai Cuisine, 101 Shopping, 102/3 Masks, 105 Dancing, 106 Muay-Thai, 108 Bull-fight, 109 Kite flying, 111 Crocodile farm Samut Prakan, 114 War Elephant Parade, 115 Traffic, 116 Thai Airways, 118/9 Currency, 120/1 Salutation, 123 Transport.

TOURIST AUTHORITY OF THAILAND 47 Hill Top People, 58 Old Sukhothai, 112/3 Candle Dance.

Author's Acknowledgements:
The following people are thanked for their assistance:
Mr Taweewat Smitabhindu (TAT London), Mr Pannara Choochan (TAT Marketing Bangkok), Ms Piyavat Songkhao (TAT Chief Reception Bangkok) and Mrs Chirisuda Vuttigrai, Public Relations Manager of the Regent Bangkok. The Regent Bangkok, Imperial Group of Hotels, Oriental and Royal Cliff Beach Resort are also thanked for their hospitality.